dance your dreams

A Kids Guide to Becoming a Dancer

sarah michaels

Copyright © 2023 by Sarah Michaels

All rights reserved.

No part of this book may be reproduced in any form or by any electronic or mechanical means, including information storage and retrieval systems, without written permission from the author, except for the use of brief quotations in a book review.

contents

Introduction	5
1. DISCOVERING DANCE	15
Different Dance Forms	15
History of Dance	19
Inspirational Stories	22
2. GETTING STARTED	27
First Steps	27
Setting Goals	31
Finding a Dance School/Class	34
3. DANCE GEAR AND PREPARATION	39
Essential Gear	39
Preparation at Home	45
4. DANCE TECHNIQUES AND FUNDAMENTALS	51
Basic Steps and Movements	51
Musicality and Rhythm	54
Posture and Alignment	58
5. OVERCOMING CHALLENGES	63
Dealing with Frustration and Setbacks	63
Physical Challenges	66
Emotional Support	70
6. PERFORMANCE SKILLS	75
Stage Presence	75
Connecting with the Audience: Techniques to engage and captivate an audience	81

7. CONNECTING WITH THE AUDIENCE - CAPTURING HEARTS AND IMAGINATIONS — 83

8. GROWTH AND DEVELOPMENT — 91
   Improving Your Skills — 91
   Attending Workshops and Camps — 96
   Learning from Others — 101

9. THE WORLD OF DANCE OPPORTUNITIES — 107
   Competitions and Performances — 107
   Dance in Education — 110
   Career Paths — 113

10. STAYING HEALTHY AND FIT — 117
    Nutrition for Dancers — 117
    Fitness and Cross-training — 121
    Mental Health — 126

11. YOUR UNIQUE DANCE JOURNEY — 133

12. SETTING LONG-TERM GOALS - DREAM BIG AND DANCE TOWARDS YOUR FUTURE — 137
    Staying Inspired — 141

    Conclusion: The Dance Continues — 145
    Appendices — 159

introduction

purpose of the book

This isn't just any book; it's your personal guide and best friend on the journey to becoming the dancer you dream to be. Whether you love twirling in your room, tapping your feet to every beat, or have just thought about dancing, this is the perfect place for you.

Dance, as you might know, is more than just moving to music. It's a way of expressing yourself, telling a story, and experiencing a kind of magic that words can't always describe. But where do you start? How do you move from tapping your toes to performing on a stage? That's where this book comes in!

Why Dance?

Introduction

First off, let's talk about why dance is so amazing. Dance is a language spoken by everyone around the world, no matter their age or where they come from. It connects people, expresses emotions, and most of all, it's super fun! Dancing can make you feel joyful, powerful, and sometimes even a little bit nervous, but above all, it gives you the freedom to be yourself.

And guess what? You already are a dancer. Every time you move to the rhythm of a song, you're dancing. This book will just help you learn some new moves, understand different dance styles, and most importantly, boost your confidence.

Your Guide on the Dance Floor

Think of this book as your personal guide on the dance floor. Just like a dance instructor, I'll be here to show you the steps, encourage you when things get tough, and celebrate every little victory with you. We're going to explore various dance styles, from the elegant swirls of ballet to the energetic moves of hip-hop, and everything in between.

We'll also meet some incredible dancers who started just like you, with a dream and a love for dancing. They faced challenges, worked hard, and kept going, and now, they dance on some of the

Introduction

biggest stages in the world. Their stories will inspire you to follow your own dance dreams.

Learning the Moves

Dance is a beautiful blend of art and skill. In this book, you'll learn about the basic moves and techniques that form the foundation of any great dancer. But remember, it's not just about the steps. Dance is also about creativity, passion, and expressing yourself. So, while you'll learn the 'hows', you'll also explore the 'whys' – why we dance and why it makes us feel so good.

We'll dive into fun activities, practice routines, and little challenges to help you improve. These aren't just exercises; they're stepping stones on your path to becoming a wonderful dancer.

Overcoming Stage Fright

It's normal to feel nervous, especially when trying something new. Stage fright is something every dancer faces, no matter how experienced they are. This book will share secrets on how to conquer those jitters and shine confidently, whether you're dancing in your living room, in a class, or on a big, bright stage.

Keeping the Spark Alive

We all have days when we feel like we're not improving, or when learning a new step feels impossible. That's perfectly okay! Dancing is a

Introduction

journey with ups and downs. This book will be your cheerleader, reminding you to be patient with yourself and to find joy in every movement, even on the tough days.

Your Dance Community

You're not alone on this journey. There's a whole world of dancers out there – beginners, pros, and everyone in between. This book will help you connect with that community, find support, make friends, and share your love for dance. You'll see that every dancer's path is unique, and that's what makes it so exciting.

Dancing into the Future

What does it mean to be a dancer? Is it performing on a big stage? Teaching others? Or just dancing for the love of it? This book will help you explore all these possibilities. We'll talk about how to set goals, improve your skills, and even how dance can be a part of your future.

It's All About You

Remember, this is your dance journey. There's no right or wrong way to be a dancer. Whether you want to perform on Broadway, make up your own dances in your backyard, or just learn a few moves to impress your friends, this book is here to support you.

And the most important thing? Have fun!

Dance is about joy, expression, and letting your heart sing through your movements. So put on your dancing shoes (or don't, barefoot is great too!) and get ready to step into the amazing world of dance.

dance story

Have you ever had a dream so big that it felt like it was bursting out of you? That's how Emily felt about dancing. She was just like any of you – a regular kid with a gigantic dream. This is her story, a story that might feel a bit like your own.

Emily lived in a small town where the biggest event was the annual summer fair. She was twelve years old, with a head full of wild curls and a heart full of rhythms that nobody else seemed to hear. At school, she was known as the girl who couldn't sit still because she was always tapping her feet or swaying to some silent melody.

Her love for dance started on a rainy Thursday afternoon when she was seven. She stumbled upon an old dance movie on TV. It was one of those black-and-white films where everyone seemed to float rather than walk. She was mesmerized. From that day on, her dream was to become a dancer.

However, Emily's journey wasn't easy. For

Introduction

starters, there weren't many opportunities to learn dance in her town. The only dance studio was on the other side of town and her family couldn't afford the classes. But Emily didn't let that stop her. She turned her small bedroom into her personal dance studio, moving the furniture aside and practicing moves she learned from online videos.

Every evening, after finishing her homework and helping her mom with dinner, Emily would jump into her 'studio' and dance. She tried everything – from hip-hop moves she saw in music videos to elegant ballet poses she copied from library books. The feeling of her heart pounding in her chest, her feet moving in rhythm, and her entire body expressing what words couldn't, was magical to her.

Emily's parents were supportive, but they were also realistic. They worried about her future, knowing the life of a dancer could be uncertain and difficult. Her dad often said, "Dancing is a fine hobby, Emily, but you need a real plan for your future." Emily understood their concerns, but inside her heart, the dream of dancing on a big stage never faded.

The big turning point came when her school announced a talent show. Emily saw it as her big chance to show everyone her passion for dance.

Introduction

She spent weeks preparing, choosing the perfect song and choreographing her routine. Every night, she practiced tirelessly, often dancing until her feet ached.

As the day of the talent show approached, Emily's excitement was tinged with nerves. She had never performed in front of such a large audience. On the night of the show, backstage, she felt her hands shake and her stomach twist into knots. What if she forgot her moves? What if people laughed? Taking a deep breath, she peeked from behind the curtains and saw her parents in the front row, her mom's encouraging smile giving her a bit of courage.

When her name was announced, she stepped onto the stage, the bright lights making her momentarily blind. As her music started, she took another deep breath and let her body take over. As she danced, something amazing happened. The audience's chatter faded, her nervousness melted away, and it was just her and the music. She spun, leaped, and flowed across the stage, her heart soaring with every move.

As the music ended, there was a brief moment of silence before the auditorium erupted into applause. Emily stood there, panting and wide-eyed, as the audience clapped and cheered. She had

Introduction

done it! She had shared her love for dance with others and they had loved it. That night, she didn't just win the talent show; she won the belief in her dream.

After the talent show, things started to change for Emily. Her parents saw her dedication and arranged for her to take classes at the local dance studio. She began to learn formally, embracing every style with enthusiasm. Ballet, jazz, contemporary – she loved them all.

Dancing wasn't always easy. There were days when Emily felt like she wasn't improving, and other days when she wondered if she was good enough. But she remembered the feeling of dancing on the talent show stage and pushed through.

Emily's dream of becoming a dancer was more alive than ever. She began participating in more shows, contests, and even got a part in the local production of "The Nutcracker." Every opportunity to dance was a step closer to her dream.

And you know what? Her journey is still ongoing. Each day is a new step, a new learning experience, and a chance to dance her heart out. She may not know exactly where her passion for dance will take her, but she's determined to follow it wherever it leads.

Emily's story is a reminder that dreams are

Introduction

powerful. They may start small, just like a seed, but with love, effort, and a bit of courage, they can grow into something extraordinary. Remember, every great dancer started somewhere – with a dream and a love for dance, just like you.

Like Emily, you too can chase your dreams of dancing. It doesn't matter where you start; what matters is that you take the step and dance. Keep moving, keep dreaming, and who knows? One day, you might just find yourself dancing under the bright lights of your own big stage.

1 / discovering dance

different dance forms

JUST LIKE THERE are countless flavors of ice cream, there are many, many styles of dance. Each one is unique, with its own moves, music, and history. Today, let's embark on a journey through some of these fascinating dance styles!

Ballet - The Graceful Art

Imagine dancers in tutus, moving gracefully on the tips of their toes. That's ballet! Originating in the Italian Renaissance courts of the 15th century, ballet is a highly technical form of dance with its own vocabulary. It's known for its precise movements, formalized steps and gestures, and ethereal quality.

Ballet dancers train for years to build strength,

flexibility, and technique. This style is often considered the backbone of dance training because it's a great foundation for other dance forms. When you watch ballet, you might feel like you're in a fairy tale, with stories told through fluid movements and emotional expressions.

Hip-Hop - The Rhythmic Street Dance

Now, let's jump into something completely different - hip-hop! This energetic dance style started in the 1970s in the streets of New York City, particularly in African American and Latino communities. It includes a variety of styles like breaking, locking, and popping.

Hip-hop is all about rhythm, personal style, and expression. It's often danced to hip-hop music and includes freestyling, where dancers improvise moves on the spot. This style is super fun, full of energy, and a great way to express yourself.

Contemporary - The Modern Emotional Journey

Contemporary dance is like a story told through movements. It began in the mid-20th century and is a blend of ballet, modern, and other dance forms. It often focuses on emotions and storytelling, with dancers using fluid movements to convey a narrative or express complex emotions.

Contemporary dance can be powerful and moving, leaving both the dancer and the audience feeling deeply connected to the performance. It's a style that encourages creativity and personal expression, making it a favorite among many dancers.

Jazz - The Lively and Energetic Beat

Picture high kicks, turns, and lots of sass – that's jazz! Jazz dance originated from African American dance forms and was popularized in the jazz clubs of the 1920s. It's known for its rhythmic, energetic movements and the use of improvisation.

Jazz dance can be seen on Broadway, in musicals, and in films. It's a fun, upbeat style that often tells a story or conveys a certain mood. Jazz dancers are usually full of energy, showing off their flexibility and rhythm.

Tap - The Rhythmic Footwork

Do you love making noise with your feet? Then tap dance might just be your thing! Originating in the United States, tap dance is characterized by using the sounds of tap shoes striking the floor as a form of percussion. It combines elements of African-American dance, English clog dancing, and Irish stepdance.

Tap dancers use their feet like drums to create rhythmic patterns and timely beats. It's a fun way to develop musicality and rhythm, and there's something really satisfying about creating music with your feet!

Traditional and Cultural Dances - The Heritage Movements

Every culture in the world has its own traditional dance. These dances are rich in history and often tell stories about a country's heritage. From the elegant Indian Bharatanatyam to the spirited Irish stepdance, traditional dances are a beautiful expression of cultural identity and history.

These dances are not just about steps or movements; they're about preserving and sharing the heritage and stories of a culture. Learning about traditional dances can be a great way to understand and appreciate the diversity of our world.

Ballroom - The Elegant Partnership

Now, let's waltz our way into the world of ballroom dancing. Ballroom dance includes styles like the waltz, tango, and cha-cha. It's unique because it's usually performed in pairs, making coordination and partnership key components.

Ballroom dancing can be both competitive and social. It's about elegance, posture, and smooth, flowing movements. When you watch ballroom dancers, you can almost feel the connection and communication between the partners – it's truly beautiful!

Every dance style has something special to offer, and there's a world of moves and rhythms waiting for you to explore. Whether you want the disciplined grace of ballet, the rhythmic soul of hip-hop, the expressive storytelling of contemporary, or the lively beats of jazz and tap, there's a dance form out there for you.

history of dance

Dance isn't just a series of steps or movements; it's a living, breathing storybook of our past. It's been a part of human culture since the dawn of time, evolving with us, telling our stories, and expressing our emotions. Let's time-travel together and see how dance has twirled its way through history.

The Ancient Beginnings

Our story begins thousands of years ago. Can you imagine ancient humans dancing? They did! Dance has been around since the earliest human civilizations. In ancient cultures, dance was more than just entertainment; it was a vital part of rituals, ceremonies, and celebrations. Whether it was to celebrate a successful hunt, invoke rain, or honor gods, dance played a crucial role.

Ancient Egyptians used dance in religious ceremonies and royal courts. Paintings in tombs show dancers in various poses, telling us that dance was an important part of their culture.

The Classical Moves of Greece and Rome

Fast forward to ancient Greece and Rome, where dance became more structured. The Greeks incorporated dance into their theater, using it to tell stories and express emotions. The Romans, on the other hand, were fond of grand dance spectacles, often featuring in their lavish festivals and events.

The Middle Ages and the Renaissance: A Changing Dance Scene

In the Middle Ages, dance took a different turn. It was often frowned upon by the church, but that didn't stop people from dancing! Folk dances were popular among common folks, a way for them to celebrate and come together.

Then came the Renaissance, a time of reawakening in art, culture, and, yes, dance! This is when ballet began to take shape. It started in the Italian courts as a form of entertainment and quickly spread to France, thanks to Catherine de Medici, an Italian noblewoman who became the queen of France. Ballet became the sophisticated dance we know today during this era, with elaborate performances and a structured technique.

The 18th and 19th Centuries: The Rise of Modern Ballet and Ballroom Dancing

As we move into the 18th and 19th centuries, ballet continued to evolve. This period saw the rise of what we call 'classical ballet.' It was during this time that iconic ballets like "Swan Lake" and "The Nutcracker" were created.

Meanwhile, in the ballrooms of Europe, social dances like the waltz and polka were all the rage. These dances were more than just leisure; they were an important part of social life, a way for people to mingle, show off their status, and, for some, to find a romantic partner.

The 20th Century: A Dance Revolution

The 20th century was like a dance explosion – so many styles emerged and evolved! This was the century that saw the birth of modern dance, with pioneers like Isadora Duncan and Martha Graham breaking away from the rigid structures of ballet to explore more free and expressive movement.

In the roaring 1920s, jazz and swing dancing took the spotlight. The Charleston, the Lindy Hop, and later the Jitterbug had people swinging and hopping in dance halls across America.

But wait, there's more! The latter half of the 20th century brought us rock and roll, disco dancing in the 1970s (think "Saturday Night Fever"), and the emergence of hip-hop culture in the 1980s with breakdancing.

The Global Dance Scene of the 21st Century

Now, we're dancing in the 21st century, a time when all these dance forms coexist and continue to evolve. Today, we have TV shows dedicated to dance, YouTube channels where you can learn any dance style, and a global community of dancers connected through the internet.

Dance today is incredibly diverse. Ballet continues to enchant audiences, hip-hop keeps evolving, contemporary dance pushes boundaries, and cultural dances from around the world gain international recognition. We also see the fusion of different styles, creating exciting new forms of dance.

inspirational stories

Just like you, they had a beginning, a moment when they first fell in love with dance. Their journeys are full of challenges, triumphs, and, most importantly, a passion for dance. Let's take a leap into the stories of some iconic dancers and see what inspiration we can find in their incredible journeys.

Misty Copeland - Breaking Barriers in Ballet

Misty Copeland's story is one of determination and breaking boundaries. She didn't start ballet until she was 13, which is quite late for a professional dancer. Growing up in a struggling family, Misty's first ballet class was on a basketball court at a local Boys & Girls Club.

Despite her late start, Misty's talent was undeniable. She was a natural, and her teachers were amazed by her rapid progress. However, her journey wasn't easy. Misty faced challenges, including injuries and being told that her body type wasn't right for ballet. But she didn't let that stop her.

In 2007, she became the second African American female soloist at the prestigious American Ballet Theatre, and in 2015, she made history by becoming the first African American woman to be promoted to principal dancer in the company's 75-year history. Misty's story shows that it's never too late to start, and with hard work and belief in yourself, you can overcome any obstacle.

Fred Astaire - The Man Who Made Dance Look Effortless

Fred Astaire, known for his smooth and elegant dance style, made dancing look effortless. But don't be fooled - behind that grace was a lot of hard work. Astaire started dancing when he was just four years old, performing in vaudeville with his sister, Adele.

His journey to stardom wasn't straightforward.

When he first went to Hollywood, a famous report stated, "Can't act. Can't sing. Slightly balding. Can dance a little." Astaire proved them wrong, becoming one of the most celebrated dancers and actors in Hollywood. He worked tirelessly to perfect his craft, rehearsing for hours to ensure every movement was flawless. His dedication and commitment to dance are truly inspiring.

Martha Graham - The Mother of Modern Dance

Martha Graham's story is about daring to be different. She didn't fit the mold of a traditional dancer; her movements were sharp, angular, and full of raw emotion. Martha started studying dance when she was a teenager, which was also considered late. She was inspired by the expressive possibilities of dance and wanted to use it to tell stories and express deep emotions.

Martha founded her own dance company in 1926, creating a radical new language of movement. Her innovative approach to dance inspired countless other artists. She danced well into her seventies and choreographed until her death at age 96, leaving behind a legacy that changed the dance world forever.

Gene Kelly - Bringing Dance to the People

Gene Kelly is known for bringing dance to the people with his charismatic and athletic style.

Unlike the more refined style of Fred Astaire, Kelly's approach was grounded, energetic, and relatable. He believed that dance should be accessible to everyone.

Kelly started dancing at a young age to help him escape the rough neighborhoods he grew up in. He faced ridicule for being a male dancer, but he persevered. He went on to star in and choreograph some of the most beloved movie musicals, including "Singin' in the Rain." Kelly's style and approach made dance something that everyone could enjoy and appreciate.

Michael Jackson - The King of Pop and Dance Innovator

While not a traditional dancer, Michael Jackson's impact on dance is undeniable. He started his music and dance career with his brothers in the Jackson 5 when he was only six years old. Jackson brought a new level of artistry to his performances, integrating dance into his music in ways that had never been seen before.

His iconic moonwalk, electric energy on stage, and groundbreaking music videos inspired a whole generation of dancers and artists. Jackson showed the world how dance could be an integral part of storytelling in music and influenced styles like hip-hop and street dance.

Each of these dancers started with a dream, a passion for dance. They faced their own set of challenges, but their love for dance kept them going. They remind us that success in dance isn't just about talent; it's also about perseverance, hard work, and, most importantly, the courage to follow your dreams.

2 / getting started

first steps

MAYBE YOU'VE BEEN DREAMING about dancing after watching a breathtaking ballet or an energetic hip-hop performance. Or perhaps, you just want to try something new and exciting. Whatever your reason, welcome to the wonderful world of dance! This chapter is all about taking those first steps and finding the dance style that makes your heart beat a little faster.

Taking the Plunge into Dance

Starting something new can feel a bit scary, but it's also thrilling! The first step is often the hardest, but once you take it, you're on your way to an amazing adventure. Let's explore how to get started and find the dance style that feels just right for you.

Explore Different Dance Styles

There are so many dance styles out there – from the gracefulness of ballet to the rhythmic beats of hip-hop, the elegant swirls of ballroom, or the expressive movements of contemporary dance. Each style has its own flavor, and trying a few can help you discover what you enjoy most.

Think about what kind of music you like, what kind of movements make you feel happy, and what challenges you want to take on. Love the idea of floating across the stage in a tutu? Ballet might be your calling. Can't sit still when a hip-hop track plays? Hip-hop dance classes could be a blast for you.

Finding the Right Dance Class

Once you have an idea of what style you might like, it's time to find a dance class. You can start by checking out local dance studios or community centers. Many offer a variety of classes and sometimes even free trial classes, so you can dip your toes in without a big commitment.

Don't forget to talk to your dance teacher before or after class. They can give you tips, help you understand what to expect, and answer any questions you might have. Remember, every dancer was a beginner once, even your teacher!

Getting Equipped

Different dance styles might require different gear. Ballet often needs ballet shoes and comfortable, form-fitting clothing, while hip-hop is more about loose clothes and sneakers. Don't worry about getting everything perfect right away. Start with the basics and add on as you go.

The First Dance Class

Your first dance class might feel a bit overwhelming, but that's perfectly normal. You'll be learning lots of new things – from the basic steps to how to move your body in new ways. It's okay to feel a bit clumsy at first; everyone does! The important thing is to have fun and keep trying.

Listen closely to your teacher, and don't be afraid to ask questions. Watch and learn from your classmates too. Remember, everyone is there to learn, just like you.

Practice, Practice, Practice

Practice is key in dance. The more you practice, the more comfortable you'll become with the movements. And as you practice, you'll start to develop your own style and flavor. You can practice at home, in the park, or anywhere you have a bit of space. Just be safe and make sure you're practicing correctly to avoid any injuries.

Patience and Perseverance

Learning to dance is a journey, and like any journey, it has its ups and downs. Some days you'll feel like you're flying, and other days it might feel like you're stuck. That's all part of the process. The important thing is to keep going, be patient with yourself, and enjoy each step along the way.

Embracing the Dance Community

Dance isn't just about the steps or the music; it's also about the people you meet along the way. The dance community can be incredibly supportive and inspiring. Make friends in your dance class, go to dance events, or join a dance club at school. Being part of a community can make your dance journey even more fulfilling.

Finding Your Dance Path

As you explore, learn, and grow in dance, you'll start to find your path. Maybe you'll fall in love with one style, or maybe you'll enjoy combining different styles. The beauty of dance is that it's a personal journey. It's about expressing who you are and finding joy in movement.

Remember, every dancer's journey is unique. There's no right or wrong way to start, and there's no limit to where you can go. The world of dance is full of possibilities, and it's all waiting for you. Lace up those dance shoes, step into the studio, and let the adventure begin! Keep dancing, exploring, and enjoying every step of the journey. Who knows what amazing places dance will take you!

setting goals

Think of goal-setting as creating a dance routine: each step is planned to make the whole performance dazzling. In the same way, setting goals in dancing helps you focus your efforts and turn your dreams into reality. Let's break down the steps to setting meaningful and fun dance goals.

Why Set Goals in Dancing?

Imagine going on a road trip without a map. You might have a great time exploring, but you could also miss some amazing destinations. That's where goals come in – they're like your dance map, guiding you to exciting places in your dance adventure. Goals help you stay motivated, track your progress, and keep the fun and excitement alive in your dancing.

Discovering What You Really Want

Before you set any goals, take a moment to think about why you love dancing. Is it the thrill of performing on stage? The joy of learning new moves? Or maybe the challenge of mastering a difficult routine? Your reasons for dancing can guide you in setting goals that are meaningful to you.

Short-Term vs. Long-Term Goals

Goals come in different sizes. Short-term goals are like the steps in a dance routine – small and achievable moves that lead to something bigger. Long-term goals are like the grand finale of a performance – the big, exciting moments you're working towards. Both are important in keeping your dance journey interesting and rewarding.

For example, a short-term goal might be to learn a new dance routine in a month, while a long-term goal could be to perform in a dance recital or competition.

SMART Goals for Dance

Have you heard of SMART goals? They're Specific, Measurable, Achievable, Relevant, and Time-bound. Let's use SMART to set some dance goals!

Specific: Be clear about what you want to achieve. Instead of saying, "I want to get better at dancing," try, "I want to learn the entire choreography of my favorite dance song."

Measurable: How will you know when you've reached your goal? Maybe you can measure it by being able to perform the routine without mistakes.

Achievable: Your goals should challenge you but still be possible to achieve. If you're just starting out, don't set a goal to win a national dance competition next month. Start with something more within reach, like mastering the basics of a dance style.

Relevant: Your goals should matter to you and align with your broader aspirations in dance. If you love hip-hop, setting a goal to learn a classical ballet piece might not feel very relevant to you.

Time-bound: Give yourself a deadline. It can be in a few weeks, months, or even a year. Just like a dance performance has a set date, your goals should have a timeline.

Writing Down Your Goals

There's power in writing down your goals. It makes them feel more real, like a promise you're making to yourself. Keep them where you can see them – on your wall, in a journal, or in a place where you practice your dancing.

Flexibility in Your Goals

It's okay if your goals change over time. Maybe you'll discover a new style of dance you want to explore, or maybe some goals will take a little longer to achieve than you thought. Just like dancing, goal-setting is flexible. Adjust your goals as you grow and learn.

Sharing Your Goals

Talking about your goals with friends, family, or your dance teacher can be super helpful. They can offer support, advice, and even join you in some of your dance goals. Plus, sharing your goals makes them feel even more real and exciting!

Celebrating Your Achievements

Every time you reach a goal, celebrate! Whether it's perfecting a tricky dance move, performing in front of an audience, or just not giving up even when it got tough – every achievement is worth celebrating. Your dance journey should be full of these little moments of triumph.

Reflecting and Looking Forward

As you achieve your goals, take some time to reflect. What did you learn? What was challenging, and how did you overcome it? Reflecting helps you appreciate how far you've come and guides you in setting new, exciting goals.

finding a dance school/class

Embarking on your dance journey is super exciting, but you might be wondering, "Where do I even begin?" Well, finding the right dance class and teacher is a great starting point! This chapter is all about helping you choose a dance school or class that fits you like a glove – or, in this case, like the perfect pair of dance shoes!

Why Choosing the Right Class and Teacher Matters

Imagine trying to learn a new dance in shoes that don't fit well. It would be pretty tough, right? The same goes for your dance class and teacher. The right fit can make learning to dance an amazing experience, while the wrong fit could make it less enjoyable. Let's twirl into some tips for finding your perfect dance match!

What Style of Dance Interests You?

First things first: what dance style makes your heart race? Ballet, hip-hop, jazz, tap, contemporary… there are so many to choose from! If you're not sure yet, that's okay! Some schools offer a mix of styles in beginner classes, so you can try a bit of everything.

Research Dance Schools and Studios

Now it's time for some detective work. Start by researching dance schools or studios in your area. You can do this online, ask friends or family, or check out local community boards. Look for schools that offer classes in the style of dance you're interested in.

Visiting the Schools

If possible, visit the dance schools you're interested in. This is a great way to get a feel for the environment. Is the studio bright and welcoming? Are the staff friendly? How about the other students – do they seem happy and engaged? The vibe of a place can tell you a lot.

Trial Classes

Many dance schools offer trial classes, which are like sneak peeks into what regular classes would be like. This is a fantastic opportunity to try out a class without committing to an entire term. See how you feel during and after the class. Did you have fun? Did you learn something new?

The Importance of a Good Teacher

A good teacher can make all the difference in your dance journey. When trying out a class, observe how the teacher interacts with the students. Are they encouraging and patient? Do they make the class fun and engaging? A teacher who makes you feel comfortable and excited to learn is a gem.

Class Size Matters

The size of the class can affect how much individual attention you get from the teacher. If you're just starting out, you might prefer smaller classes where the teacher can give more personalized guidance.

Your Dance Goals

Remember those goals you set? Keep them in mind when choosing a dance class. If you're aiming to become a competitive dancer, you might look for a school with a strong focus on technique and performance. If you're dancing just for fun and fitness, a more relaxed class might be perfect for you.

Check Out the Facilities

Take a look around the school's facilities. Do they have proper dance floors that are safe to dance on? Are the spaces clean and well-maintained? The right environment can enhance your learning experience.

Ask Questions

Don't be shy to ask questions! Talk to the teachers or school administrators. Find out about class schedules, fees, dress codes, and any performances or recitals. The more information you have, the better your decision will be.

Consider Your Schedule and Budget

Dancing should fit into your life comfortably. Consider how often classes are held and if they fit with your school schedule. Also, think about the cost. Dance can be an investment, so it's important to find a class that fits your family's budget.

Listen to Your Gut

Sometimes, the best guide is your own intuition. If a class or school just feels right, it probably is! Trust your feelings. After all, dance is all about expressing yourself.

The Journey of a Thousand Dances Begins with a Single Step

Remember, finding the right dance school or class is just the beginning of your adventure. Each step, spin, and leap you learn is a part of your unique dance story.

3 /
dance gear and preparation

essential gear

NOW THAT YOU'RE on your way to becoming a dancing superstar, let's talk about something super important – your dance gear! Just like a superhero needs their cape, a dancer needs the right gear to perform their best. In this chapter, we'll dive into the world of dancewear, shoes, and accessories for various dance styles. Ready to gear up? Let's go!

Why the Right Gear Matters

Imagine trying to tap dance in sneakers or ballet in boots – it wouldn't work very well, right? Each dance style has specific gear that not only looks cool but also helps you dance better and safer. The right shoes can help you glide smoothly, turn effortlessly, and even protect your feet from injuries. The same goes for dancewear and accessories. Plus, dressing the part can make you feel more like a real dancer, boosting your confidence as you step onto the dance floor.

Gear for Different Dance Styles

Each dance style has its own unique flair, and the gear you need varies from one style to another. Let's explore what you might wear for different types of dance:

Ballet:

Leotard and Tights: Ballet dancers usually wear a leotard and tights. Leotards come in many styles and colors, but most beginners start with a simple black or pink one. Tights help protect your legs and are either pink or skin-toned.

Ballet Shoes: These are soft, lightweight shoes that help you feel the floor and perfect your technique. They're usually pink or white and have a snug fit.

Ballet Skirts: Some dancers wear a ballet skirt, especially in performances. These are often light and floaty, adding elegance to your movements.

Hair Accessories: Ballet often requires neat hair, usually in a bun. Hairnets, bobby pins, and hair ties are essentials in a ballet dancer's bag.

Hip-Hop:

Comfortable Clothing: Hip-hop is all about attitude and comfort. Loose pants or joggers, and a comfortable t-shirt or tank top work well.

Sneakers: Durable sneakers with good support are key for hip-hop. Look for shoes with a smooth sole to help with sliding and turning.

Accessories: Feel free to express your style with cool hats, bandanas, or even colorful hair ties.

Jazz:

. . .

Jazz Pants and Tops: Like hip-hop, jazz dance is about comfort and style. Many dancers wear jazz pants, which are tight at the thigh and flared at the bottom, paired with a snug top.

Jazz Shoes: These are similar to ballet shoes but often have a small heel and a split sole for flexibility.

Hair Accessories: Since jazz involves a lot of movement, keeping your hair out of your face is important. Headbands or clips are great options.

Tap:

Comfortable Outfits: Most tap dancers wear comfortable clothes that allow for easy movement. This could be anything from leggings and a t-shirt to a more traditional leotard and tights.

Tap Shoes: The stars of tap dancing! These shoes have metal plates on the bottom that create the signature tapping sound. They come in various styles and sizes.

Contemporary:

• • •

Flowy Garments: Contemporary dance often uses the movement of the clothing as part of the dance. Flowy dresses, skirts, or loose pants are common.

Barefoot or Contemporary Shoes: Many contemporary dancers perform barefoot to connect more with the floor. There are also special contemporary shoes that are very thin and flexible.

Taking Care of Your Gear

Just like any superhero would take care of their cape, it's important to take care of your dance gear. Keep your shoes clean and dry them out properly after class (no stinky feet, please!). Wash your dancewear according to the instructions, and keep everything neatly packed in your dance bag.

Where to Buy Dance Gear

You can find dance gear at specialty dance shops or online. If you're not sure about your size, especially for shoes, it's a good idea to visit a store so you can try things on. Some dance schools also have their own shops or recommendations for where to buy gear.

Customizing Your Gear

One of the fun parts of dance is expressing your personality. Once you have the basics, feel free to add your own flair! Maybe it's a cool headband for jazz class or colorful leg warmers for ballet. Just make sure it's okay with your dance teacher and suitable for the dance style.

Budget-Friendly Tips

Dance gear can sometimes be pricey, but don't worry – there are budget-friendly options! Look for second-hand gear, consider gear swaps with other dancers, or check out sales and discounts at dance stores.

preparation at home

Let's chat about something super important - preparing to dance, not just in the studio, but right at home! Imagine you're a rocket about to launch into space; you need to warm up your engines first, right? The same goes for dancing. Before you show off your cool moves, you need to stretch, warm up, and practice. Ready to learn how? Here we go!

Why Stretching and Warming Up is Important

Before you jump into dancing, it's important to prepare your body. Stretching and warming up reduce the chance of injuries, like strains or sprains, and help your muscles work better. Plus, they make you more flexible, which is a superpower in the dance world!

Stretching Like a Pro

. . .

Sarah Michaels

Stretching is all about gently pulling your muscles to make them longer and more flexible. Here are some key stretches you can do:

Toe Touches: Stand up, keep your legs straight, and reach down towards your toes. Feel the stretch at the back of your legs? That's your hamstrings saying thank you!

Butterfly Stretch: Sit down, bend your knees, and put the soles of your feet together. Gently press your knees down with your elbows. This helps your hip muscles.

Arm Stretches: Reach one arm across your body and use the other arm to pull it closer. Then, take one arm over your head, bend it at the elbow, and push gently on the elbow with your other hand. This helps your shoulders and arms.

Remember, stretching should never hurt. If it does, ease up a bit.

· · ·

Dance Your Dreams

Warming Up Your Body

Warming up is like telling your body, "Hey, we're about to dance!" It gets your blood flowing and muscles ready. Here are some fun warm-up ideas:

Jogging in Place: Jog for a few minutes in your room or backyard. It gets your heart rate up and muscles warm.

Jumping Jacks: These are great for overall warming up. Do a couple of sets, and you'll feel your energy level soar!

Dance to Your Favorite Song: Nothing warms you up like dancing freely to a song you love. Let loose and have fun with it!

Practicing Dance at Home

. . .

Practicing at home helps you improve faster and lets you explore your own style. Here's how you can practice effectively:

Create a Dance Space: Find a little space in your home where you can move freely. Make sure it's safe – no slippery floors or sharp objects around.

Use a Mirror: If you can, practice in front of a mirror. It's a great way to check your posture and movements.

Repetition is Key: Practice your dance moves repeatedly. The more you do it, the better you get.

Record Yourself: Sometimes, record your dance and watch it. It's a cool way to see your progress and notice areas you can improve.

Balancing School and Dance

. . .

Remember, being a great dancer also means balancing your dance practice with schoolwork and rest. Make a schedule that includes time for homework, dancing, and relaxation. Your brain and body will thank you for it!

Taking Breaks and Staying Hydrated

While practicing, don't forget to take short breaks and drink water. Staying hydrated is super important for dancers. Your body is like a sponge; it needs water to stay flexible and strong.

Safety Tips for Home Practice

When practicing at home, always be mindful of safety. Make sure you have enough space, and the floor isn't slippery. If you're trying something new or difficult, maybe wait to try it in your dance class, where your teacher can guide you.

Yoga and Meditation for Dancers

· · ·

Apart from dancing, activities like yoga and meditation can be really beneficial. They improve your flexibility, balance, and even help you stay calm and focused – all great skills for a dancer!

Nutrition for Young Dancers

Eating healthy is also part of your dance preparation. Foods rich in protein, like chicken, fish, beans, and nuts, are great for muscle repair. Fruits, vegetables, and whole grains give you the energy to dance your heart out.

4 /
dance techniques and fundamentals

basic steps and movements

LET'S dive into the world of dance steps and movements. These are like the ABCs of dance, and once you get them down, you'll be writing your own dance stories in no time! Every dance style has its own set of basic steps, and we're going to explore some of the most popular ones. Ready to step into the dance floor of knowledge? Let's go!

Ballet - The Dance of Elegance

Ballet is like the queen of dance styles, known for its grace and discipline. Here are some basic ballet steps:

Plie (plee-AY): This means 'to bend'. Stand with your feet together, then bend your knees gently. It's the foundation for many ballet movements.

Tendu (tahn-DOO): From a standing position, slide one foot out to point your toe, keeping the other foot flat on the ground. It means 'to stretch'.

Pirouette (peer-WET): A spin on one foot! Start with a plie, then lift into the spin. Balance is key here.

Hip-Hop - The Cool Street Beat

Hip-hop is all about rhythm and attitude. Here are some basic steps:

The Two-Step: Just step from side to side to the beat. It's simple but crucial to get the groove of hip-hop.

The Body Wave: Move your body in a wave-like motion, starting from your head down to your toes. It's all about fluid movement.

The Running Man: It's like you're running on the spot. A fun and energetic move that always gets the crowd excited!

Contemporary - Free and Expressive

Contemporary dance blends ballet, jazz, and modern dance. It's about expressing emotion through movement. Here are some fundamental steps:

Contract and Release: This involves contracting your torso, curving forward, and then releasing back into an upright position. It's all about control and flow.

Leg Swings: Stand on one leg and swing the other from front to back. This helps with balance and flexibility.

Roll Down: Start by standing tall, then slowly roll down your spine until your hands touch the floor, and roll back up. It's great for flexibility.

Jazz - The Energetic and Fun Style

Jazz is lively, fun, and full of energy. Here are some basic steps:

Jazz Square: Imagine drawing a square with your feet. Cross one foot over the other, step back, side, and front. It's a classic!

Kick Ball Change: This is a quick move where you kick one foot forward, step on the ball of that foot, and then step your other foot down.

Jazz Hands: Okay, it's not a step, but who doesn't love jazz hands? Spread your fingers and shake those hands with energy!

Tap Dancing - Making Music with Your Feet

In tap dancing, your shoes become an instrument. Here are some basic steps:

Shuffle: Slide your foot forward, then back. The sound is made from the tap shoe hitting the floor.

Ball Change: Stand on the balls of your feet and quickly change weight between them. It's a foundational step for many tap combinations.

Flap: A step forward followed by a brush of the foot. It's like a shuffle but moving forward.

Safety and Practice

While practicing these steps, always remember to stay safe. Make sure you have enough space, and if you're not sure about a move, ask your dance teacher for help.

Mixing and Matching

One of the coolest things about dance is you can mix different styles. Try adding a hip-hop move into a contemporary routine or a ballet move into jazz. Be creative!

Remember, Practice Makes Perfect!

The key to mastering these steps is practice, practice, practice! Don't be discouraged if you don't get it right away. Even the best dancers started where you are now.

musicality and rhythm

Imagine dance as a conversation between your body and the music. When you understand this language, you can turn any tune into a beautiful dance story. Let's turn up the volume and get started!

Understanding Music Basics

First, let's tune into some music basics. Music is made up of beats, rhythm, melody, and tempo:

Beats: Think of the beat as the heart of the music. It's like a steady clock ticking, the thump-thump you might tap your foot to.

Rhythm: If the beat is a simple tap, rhythm is how those taps are arranged. It's the pattern in the music that makes you want to move.

Melody: This is the part of the music you would hum along to. It's the tune that often sticks in your head.

Tempo: Tempo is how fast or slow the music is. A fast tempo might make you want to jump around, while a slow one could make you sway gently.

Feeling the Beat

The first step in dancing to music is feeling the beat. Here's how you can practice:

Play some music and tap your foot or clap along to the beat.

Try counting "1, 2, 3, 4" with the beats.

Notice how some music makes you want to move fast, while others make you want to move slow. That's all about the tempo.

Rhythm Patterns

Different music has different rhythm patterns.

Some are steady and even, while others might have unexpected beats. Here's a fun exercise:

Listen to different songs and try clapping the rhythm. Notice how it's different from just the beat.

Try to move your body to the rhythm. Maybe sway your arms, bob your head, or stomp your feet.

Expressing the Music Through Dance

Dance is about expressing what you hear in the music. Here are some tips:

Listen to the melody: Try to let the melody guide your bigger movements. If the melody jumps high, you might leap. If it flows smoothly, you might do long, sweeping moves.

Play with dynamics: Dynamics are about the energy in your movement. If the music is soft, you can move gently. If it's loud and bold, make your movements the same.

Interpret the emotion: Music can be happy, sad, exciting, or calm. Try to express these emotions in your dance. If a song feels joyful, let your dance be full of smiles and energetic steps.

Practicing with Different Music Styles

Different styles of music will challenge you in new ways. Try these exercises:

Classical music: Focus on flowing movements and graceful expressions.

Dance Your Dreams

Hip-hop or electronic: Here, you can play with sharp, defined movements.

Jazz or swing: These styles are perfect for bouncy, lively steps.

Ballads or slow songs: Practice control and express deep emotions with your movements.

Creating Your Own Dance Routines

Once you get the hang of moving with the music, start creating your own dance routines. Pick a song you love and imagine a story you want to tell through dance. Don't worry about getting it perfect. It's all about having fun and expressing yourself.

Listening, Learning, and Growing

The best dancers are always listening and learning. Watch dance videos and see how the dancers interpret the music. Notice how a hip-hop dancer moves differently to a beat than a ballet dancer.

Musical Games and Activities

Try these fun musical activities:

Freeze Dance: Dance while the music plays, and freeze when it stops. It helps you tune into the music's start and stop.

Musical Storytelling: Pick a song and create a dance that tells a story. You can even dress up and make it a performance!

Musical Chairs with a Twist: Instead of walking

around chairs, dance around them! When the music stops, find a chair.

Remember, There's No Right or Wrong

The most important thing to remember is that there's no right or wrong way to dance to music. It's all about how the music makes you feel and how you want to express those feelings.

posture and alignment

Just like building a strong tower needs a good foundation, great dancing starts with great posture and alignment. Let's explore why this is super important and how you can perfect it!

What is Posture and Why is it Important?

Posture is how you hold your body when you're standing, sitting, or moving. Good posture is about aligning your body correctly. This isn't just for looking confident (although that's a cool bonus!), it's vital for preventing injuries, moving gracefully, and improving your dance technique.

Finding Your Perfect Posture

Let's do a quick activity to understand good posture:

Stand Up Straight: Stand with your feet hip-width apart. Imagine a string pulling you up from the top of your head, making you taller.

Align Your Spine: Try not to arch your back too much or slouch. Your spine has natural curves, and you want to keep them, not exaggerate them.

Shoulders Down and Back: Let your shoulders relax down away from your ears and gently pull them back.

Head Over Heart, Heart Over Hips: Your head should be right over your heart, and your heart should be right over your hips. This alignment helps with balance.

The Role of Core Strength

A strong core (the muscles around your belly and back) is like a secret superpower for dancers. It helps keep your posture perfect and makes movements smoother and more controlled. Here are some exercises to strengthen your core:

Plank: Like you're about to do a push-up, hold your body straight like a plank. Try holding it for 30 seconds and increase over time.

Bicycle Crunches: Lie on your back, pedal your legs in the air, and touch your opposite elbow to your knee as you pedal.

Body Alignment in Different Dance Styles

Different dance styles have different alignment focuses:

Ballet: In ballet, alignment is all about a straight spine and pulled-up posture.

Hip-Hop: Hip-hop can have a more relaxed posture, but alignment is still key for balance.

Contemporary: This style combines different alignments but always returns to a strong, centered posture.

Practice Makes Perfect

Improving your posture and alignment takes practice. Here are some tips:

Mirror, Mirror: Practice in front of a mirror. Check your alignment and correct it.

Photographic Feedback: Have someone take pictures or videos of you dancing. Look at them to see where you can improve.

Posture Checkpoints: Throughout the day, check your posture. Are you slouching while sitting? Are your shoulders creeping up when you're stressed?

Breathing and Posture

Breathing right is also a part of good posture. Deep, diaphragmatic breathing (breathing from your belly, not just your chest) helps maintain good posture and keeps you relaxed and focused.

Common Posture Mistakes in Dance

Here are some common posture mistakes to watch out for:

Slouching: Keep your back straight, not curved forward.

Overarching the Back: This can strain your back. Keep your spine's natural curve.

Tensing Shoulders: Keep them relaxed and down.

Activities for Better Posture

Let's make improving posture fun:

Balance Challenges: Try balancing on one foot. A good posture helps you stay balanced.

Posture Tag: Play a game of tag where you can only tag someone if they're not in good posture.

Benefits of Good Posture Outside of Dance

Good posture isn't just for dancing. It helps you in other sports, makes you look more confident, and keeps your body healthy and happy as you grow.

Growing with Grace

Remember, as you grow, your body changes, and so will your posture. Keep practicing, keep learning, and keep loving the journey. Dance is not just about the steps you perform; it's about how you carry yourself while doing them. Stand tall, dance proudly, and let your posture reflect the confident and amazing dancer you are becoming!

5 /
overcoming challenges

dealing with frustration and setbacks

EVERYONE, and I mean everyone, faces tough times and frustrations, even the best dancers in the world. It's like trying to learn a new dance move and not getting it right on the first, second, or even the tenth try. It can be super annoying, right? But these challenges are stepping stones to becoming an amazing dancer. Let's talk about how you can overcome these hurdles and keep your dance passion burning bright!

Understanding Frustration in Dance

Frustration in dance can come from many places. Maybe it's a dance move that's tricky, or perhaps you feel like you're not improving as fast as you'd like. It could even be that you're comparing yourself to others. Remember, feeling frustrated is totally normal. It means you care about what you're doing!

The Power of Patience and Persistence

Patience and persistence are like your secret dance power-ups. When things get tough, remind yourself why you started dancing. Love the music? Love the way dancing makes you feel? Keep those feelings close to your heart. Being patient and persistent will help you push through tough times.

Tackling the Tough Moves

Stuck on a move? Break it down into smaller parts. Work on each part slowly and then put them together. Sometimes, stepping away for a bit and coming back later helps too.

Celebrate Small Wins

Did you finally get that step right? Did you dance a whole routine without messing up? Celebrate these moments! Small victories add up and help you see how much you're actually achieving.

Learning from Mistakes

Mistakes are not just mistakes; they're lessons in disguise. Every time you mess up, you learn something new about how to do it better. Think of mistakes as your personal dance teachers.

Comparing Yourself to Others

Seeing other dancers who seem better can be tough. But remember, they were once beginners too! Instead of comparing, try to learn from them. What do they do that you admire? How can you incorporate that into your own dancing?

Setting Realistic Goals

Setting goals that are too big and too soon can lead to frustration. Instead, set smaller, achievable goals. This way, you get to experience success more often, which boosts your motivation.

Finding Support and Encouragement

You're not alone in your dance journey. Talk to your friends, family, or dance teacher when you're feeling down. Sometimes, just talking about it can make a big difference. And who knows, they might have some great advice or encouragement!

Taking Care of Your Body and Mind

Dancing is as much about your mind as it is about your body. Eating healthy foods, getting enough sleep, and doing activities that make you happy can help keep frustrations at bay.

Creative Outlets for Frustration

Feeling really stuck? Try expressing your frustration creatively. Draw, write a story, or choreograph a dance about how you're feeling. You might discover new insights or even new moves!

Remembering the Joy of Dance

Sometimes, when we're focused on getting better, we forget why we started dancing in the first place. Is it the music? The way it makes you feel free? Reconnect with that joy. Dance like nobody's watching and remember that fun.

Dealing with Negative Thoughts

Negative thoughts can sneak in and make everything seem worse. When this happens, try to replace them with positive ones. Instead of thinking, "I can't do this," try thinking, "I'm getting better every day."

Learning to Rest, Not Quit

There's a big difference between giving up and taking a break. If you're feeling really overwhelmed, it's okay to take a short break from dancing. Use this time to recharge and come back stronger.

Your Dance Journey is Unique

Your dance journey is your own, and it's going to be different from everyone else's. Embrace your unique path and celebrate your own progress.

physical challenges

While dancing is a lot of fun and super exciting, it's also a physical activity, and just like any sport, there can be bumps and bruises along the way. But don't worry! We're going to talk about common dance injuries and how to dodge them, so you can keep dancing safely and happily.

Understanding Common Dance Injuries

Dance involves a lot of movements - jumping, turning, stretching. Sometimes, these movements can cause injuries if we're not careful. Let's look at some common ones:

Sprains and Strains: These happen when muscles or ligaments are overstretched. They can be a bit painful, but with the right care, they heal.

Bruises: Everyone gets a bruise now and then, especially when learning new moves.

Tendonitis: This is when tendons (the cords connecting muscle to bone) get irritated. It's often due to overuse, like practicing the same move a lot.

Stress Fractures: These are tiny cracks in the bone from repeated stress (like a lot of jumping).

Dislocations and Fractures: These are more serious and happen when bones are forced out of place or break.

Warm-Up: Your Injury Prevention Superpower

One of the best ways to prevent injuries is a proper warm-up. Before you start dancing, take at least 10-15 minutes to get your muscles warm and ready. Jog in place, do some gentle stretches, and slowly move your body to wake it up.

Technique Matters

Good technique isn't just about looking graceful; it's also about safety. When you learn the right way to do a dance move, you're less likely to hurt yourself. Pay attention in class and don't be afraid to ask your teacher for help if you're unsure about a move.

Don't Push Too Hard

It's great to push yourself to be better, but pushing too hard can lead to injuries. Listen to your body. If something hurts, stop and rest. There's always tomorrow to try again.

The Right Gear Can Save Your Gears

Wearing the right shoes and clothes for dancing is super important. Different dance styles need different types of shoes to protect your feet. Also, make sure your clothes let you move freely and don't cause you to slip or trip.

Stay Hydrated and Eat Right

Drinking water and eating healthy foods give your body the energy it needs to dance and helps prevent injuries. Always have a water bottle handy during class and munch on fruits, veggies, and protein to keep your energy up.

Cross-Training for Strength

Other activities like swimming, yoga, or even just playing at the park can help build the strength and flexibility you need for dancing. This helps prevent injuries by making your body stronger and more adaptable.

Rest Is Not for the Weak

Rest days are important. Your body needs time to heal and recover, especially if you're practicing a lot. Make sure you get plenty of sleep and take days off from dancing to relax.

First Aid Basics

If you do get a minor injury like a sprain or bruise, the R.I.C.E method can help:

Rest: Stop dancing and rest your injured part.

Ice: Apply ice to reduce swelling and pain.

Compression: Wrap the injured area with a bandage to give it support.

Elevation: Keep the injured part raised above your heart to reduce swelling.

When to See a Doctor

If you're in a lot of pain, can't move a body part normally, or if the pain doesn't go away after a few days, it's time to see a doctor. Don't try to dance through serious pain; it can make things worse.

A Positive Mindset in Recovery

If you're dealing with an injury, it's okay to feel a bit down. But try to stay positive. Use this time to watch dance videos for inspiration, read about dance, or even work on the parts of your body that aren't injured.

Returning to Dance After an Injury

When you're feeling better and ready to dance again, take it slow. Start with gentle warm-ups and gradually increase your dancing. Listen to your body and don't rush it.

Preventing Future Injuries

Learning from past injuries can help you avoid future ones. Think about what caused your injury and talk to your teacher about ways to prevent it from happening again.

emotional support

Have you ever felt a bit nervous before a dance class or a performance? Or maybe there was a day when learning a new step felt really tough? It happens to everyone. That's where emotional support comes in – it's like a secret superpower in your dance journey. In this chapter, we'll chat about how your friends, family, and mentors can be your personal cheer squad, guiding lights, and support pillars.

Family: Your First Fans

Your family can be your biggest supporters. They're there for you from your first shuffle to your grand stage debut. Here's how they can help:

Encouragement: Those words, "You can do it!" mean a lot, especially coming from your family.

Providing Resources: Whether it's driving you to dance classes, buying dance gear, or helping you find information about dancing, their support is super helpful.

Listening Ear: After a tough day or a great practice, talking with your family can make a big difference.

Friends: Your Backstage Crew

Friends – especially those who love dancing too – can be amazing partners on your dance journey. They understand the ups and downs because they're right there with you.

Shared Experiences: Practicing together, talking about dance styles, or just laughing over a misstep, friends can make the dance journey more fun.

Encouragement and Advice: Sometimes, your friends can give you tips or encouragement that's just what you needed to hear.

Emotional Support: On days when dancing feels hard, a friend's understanding can be the best pick-me-up.

Mentors: Guiding Stars in the Dance Sky

A mentor can be a dance teacher, an older dancer, or anyone who's been on the dance journey before you. They're like a guidebook that can talk!

Sharing Knowledge: Mentors can teach you about different dance styles, techniques, and even the history of dance.

Offering Advice: Got a dance problem? Mentors have been there, done that, and can offer really useful advice.

Inspiring You: Just seeing what your mentors have achieved can be a big inspiration.

Building a Supportive Dance Community

Sometimes, the best support comes from building a community. This could be a dance club at school, a local dance group, or even an online forum for young dancers.

Connecting with Others: Meeting others who share your passion for dance can be exciting and inspiring.

Learning Together: In a community, everyone has something to share. You can learn a lot from each other.

Supporting Each Other: A dance community is like a big team, cheering for each member.

Family and Friends as Your Audience

Performing for family and friends can be a great

way to practice and build confidence. They're your personal, friendly audience, ready to applaud your every move.

Communicating with Your Supporters

Talking to your supporters about your dance goals, challenges, and successes helps them understand your journey and how they can be part of it. Remember, it's okay to tell them if you're feeling stressed or need a break, too.

Learning from Feedback

Sometimes, your supporters might have feedback or advice. Listen to what they say – it could be really helpful. If the feedback is tough to hear, try to take it positively. They want you to succeed!

Celebrating Together

When you achieve a goal – like nailing a difficult step, performing well, or just improving – celebrate with your supporters. It's a journey you're all on together, and every milestone is worth celebrating.

The Power of Encouragement

Never underestimate how powerful a simple "You did great!" can be. Encouragement from your supporters can boost your confidence and keep you motivated.

Facing Challenges Together

There will be times when dancing gets tough.

Sarah Michaels

Maybe there's a move you can't get right, or you're feeling a bit burned out. That's when your supporters can be a real anchor, helping you stay grounded and reminding you of how far you've come.

6 /
performance skills

stage presence

PICTURE THIS: You're standing backstage, the curtains are about to part, and a sea of faces waits on the other side. Exciting, right? But also, maybe a little scary? That's where stage presence comes in – it's your superpower that transforms nerves into dazzling confidence. Let's dive into the world of stage presence and learn how to own the stage!

What is Stage Presence?

Stage presence isn't just about how well you dance. It's about how you fill the space, connect with the audience, and express your emotions. It's that special something that makes people watch and remember you.

It Starts with Confidence

Building confidence is the first step. Remember, confidence doesn't mean you never get nervous. It means you believe in yourself enough to dance through those nerves.

Positive Thinking: A positive mindset goes a long way. Remind yourself of your strengths and the hard work you've put in.

Practice Makes Perfect: The more you practice, the more confident you become in your moves.

Visualize Success: Before you step onto the stage, picture yourself nailing every move. Visualization can be a powerful tool.

Body Language Speaks Volumes

. . .

The way you carry yourself can say as much as your dance moves. Let's talk about some key elements:

Posture: Stand tall, with your shoulders back and your head held high. Good posture exudes confidence.

Facial Expressions: Your face is a mirror of your emotions. Don't be afraid to express joy, passion, or intensity with your expressions.

Eye Contact: Connecting with your audience through eye contact makes your performance more engaging.

Connecting with the Music

Understanding the music is like understanding a dance partner. Let the rhythm, melody, and mood guide your movements and expressions.

Feel the Beat: Let the rhythm of the music become a part of you.

Express the Emotion: If the music is joyful, let

your happiness shine through. If it's powerful, show that strength in your movements.

Storytelling through Dance

Every dance tells a story. Your job is to bring that story to life.

Understand the Story: Whether it's a tale of love, a celebration, or a journey, know the story your dance tells.

Emotion and Expression: Use your movements and expressions to narrate the story. Make your audience feel every twist and turn.

The Power of Presence

Presence is about being in the moment and fully committing to your performance.

. . .

Focus: During a performance, let everything else fade away. Focus on your dance, your music, and your audience.

Energy: Fill the stage with your energy. Make your presence so strong that even the last row feels it.

Learning from Others

Watch performances by dancers you admire. Notice how they use their stage presence to enhance their performance. Learn from them and incorporate what you see into your own style.

Feedback and Improvement

Ask for feedback from your teachers, family, or friends. What do they think about your stage presence? Use this feedback to improve.

Dealing with Stage Fright

• • •

It's normal to feel stage fright. Even professional dancers get nervous. The key is to use that adrenaline to enhance your performance, not hinder it.

Breathing Exercises: Deep, steady breaths can calm your nerves.

Positive Reinforcement: Remind yourself of your talent and hard work.

Routine: Have a pre-performance routine to help you focus and relax.

Performance Opportunities

Look for opportunities to perform, whether it's a school talent show, a dance recital, or a community event. The more you perform, the better you'll get at channeling your stage presence.

Enjoy the Moment

Remember to have fun! Enjoy the thrill of the performance, the joy of dancing, and the applause of the audience. When you're having fun, your stage presence naturally shines brighter.

Building your stage presence is a journey, just like learning to dance. It's about confidence, connection, emotion, and storytelling. With practice, patience, and passion, you'll light up the stage every time you dance. Remember, the stage is your canvas, and you are the artist. Paint it with your unique colors of confidence and charisma. Shine on, dancers!

connecting with the audience: techniques to engage and captivate an audience

7 /
connecting with the audience - capturing hearts and imaginations

HAVE you ever watched a dancer and felt like they were dancing just for you? That's the magic of connecting with an audience! It's like a secret conversation between the dancer and the viewers, filled with emotion and storytelling. Let's explore how you can create that magical connection in your own performances.

The Power of Storytelling

Every dance is a story, and your audience loves a good tale. Think of yourself as a storyteller, using your body instead of words.

. . .

Know Your Story: Understand the story your dance is telling. Is it a joyful celebration? A powerful journey? A tale of triumph?

Express Emotion: Your emotions bring the story to life. Feel them deeply and let them shine through in your dance.

Eye Contact: A Window to the Soul

Eyes can speak volumes without saying a word. When you make eye contact with your audience, it's like you're inviting them into your world.

Scan the Audience: Instead of staring at one point, gently scan across the audience. It makes everyone feel included.

Connect, Don't Stare: A gentle, fleeting connection is more powerful than a fixed stare. Think of it as a smile with your eyes.

Facial Expressions: The Silent Communicator

· · ·

Your face can express a thousand words. A smile, a frown, or a look of determination can tell your audience how you feel.

Practice in the Mirror: Spend time in front of a mirror practicing different expressions.
Match the Mood: Your facial expressions should match the mood of the dance. A joyful dance? Smile brightly! A dramatic piece? Show intensity.

Body Language: Speaking without Words

Your body tells a story too. How you move, your posture, and your gestures all speak to the audience.

Open Gestures: Use open, expansive movements to reach out to the audience.
Confident Posture: Stand tall and proud. Confidence is contagious!

. . .

Sarah Michaels

Engaging with Emotion

Dance is an emotional experience. Let your emotions flow through your movements.

Feel the Dance: Let yourself truly feel the emotions of the dance.

Transmit Emotion: Think of your emotions as energy you're sending out to the audience.

Music: The Universal Language

Music and dance are best friends. The music sets the tone, and your dance brings it to life.

Understand the Music: Listen to the music deeply and understand its highs and lows.

Ride the Waves: Let the music guide your movements and expressions.

· · ·

Creating Moments

Some moments in a dance are special – they're the ones that stick with the audience long after the curtain falls.

Highlight Key Moments: Emphasize the most powerful moments of your dance. A dramatic leap, a gentle turn, or a powerful pose can be memorable.

Pause and Effect: Sometimes, a well-timed pause can have a huge impact.

Practice Makes Perfect

The more you perform, the better you'll become at connecting with your audience.

Perform Often: Take every opportunity to perform in front of an audience, no matter how small.

Record and Review: Record your performances

and watch them. See how your connection with the audience comes across.

Feedback is Gold

Listen to what others say about your performances. What made them feel connected? What could be improved?

Remember, They're on Your Side

Audiences generally want you to succeed. They're there to enjoy your performance, not to judge you harshly.

The Magic of Authenticity

Be true to yourself. When you're genuine, your connection with the audience becomes more natural and powerful.

· · ·

In the End, It's About Sharing Joy

Remember, at its heart, dance is about sharing joy and beauty. When you step onto the stage, you're sharing a piece of your heart. That's the ultimate connection.

8 /
growth and development

improving your skills

DANCING IS A JOURNEY, and there's always something new to learn and ways to get even better. Let's dive into some advanced techniques and super helpful practice tips to keep you improving day by day.

1. Technique Time

Balance and Control: Mastering balance is crucial. Practice balancing exercises like relevés or arabesques. It's not just about staying upright; it's about controlling your movements gracefully.

Flexibility Fun: Flexibility is your friend in dance. Work on it regularly with safe stretching exercises. Remember, never push too hard – flexibility improves over time.

Turns and Spins: These can be tricky but oh-so-impressive. Practice spotting – fixing your gaze on one point as you turn to avoid getting dizzy.

2. Strength and Stamina

Core Strength: A strong core is essential. Exercises like planks and sit-ups can really help. They're not always fun, but they are super effective!

Leg and Arm Strength: Squats, lunges, and push-ups will help build the strength needed for those amazing moves.

Building Stamina: To dance longer and stronger, cardio exercises are key. Try jogging, cycling, or even a dance-aerobics class.

3. Practice Makes Perfect

. . .

Daily Practice: Even just a little bit every day can make a huge difference. It's like adding a penny to a piggy bank – over time, you'll have a treasure!

Focus on Weak Spots: We all have them. Spend extra time working on moves that challenge you the most.

Variety is the Spice of Dance: Mix up your practice routine. Try different styles, techniques, and music to keep things interesting.

4. Advanced Moves

Leaps and Jumps: Work on height and form. Use your whole body to launch into these moves, and remember to land softly.

Turns and Pirouettes: Practice these until they feel as natural as walking. Start slow, then work your way up to multiple turns.

Expressive Hands and Feet: The details matter. Work on the finesse of your hand gestures and footwork.

5. Performance Skills

. . .

Expression: Your face tells a story as much as your body. Practice expressing emotions through your facial expressions.

Stage Presence: Own the stage. Walk on with confidence, hold your head high, and perform as if you're dancing for a crowd, even when you're alone.

6. Seeking Feedback

Teachers and Mentors: Their experience is invaluable. Listen to their advice and try to apply it.

Peer Review: Sometimes, fellow dancers can offer helpful tips. They know what you're going through!

Self-Evaluation: Record your practices and performances. Watching yourself can show you a lot about what you need to work on.

7. Learning from Others

. . .

Watch the Pros: See how professional dancers move and express themselves. You can learn a lot by observing.

Attend Workshops and Classes: These can introduce you to new techniques and styles.

Dance Collaboration: Dancing with others can push you to try new things and improve faster.

8. Nutrition and Health

Healthy Eating: Good food equals good energy. Fuel your body with nutritious foods that give you the energy you need to dance your best.

Stay Hydrated: Water is your best friend. It keeps your body functioning well and helps with muscle recovery.

9. Mental Wellness

Stay Positive: A positive mindset will keep you motivated.

Handle Criticism Constructively: Use it as a tool for improvement, not as a setback.

Rest and Relaxation: Your mind needs a break too. Give yourself time to unwind and enjoy other things you love.

10. Consistency and Commitment

Set Goals: What do you want to achieve in your dance? Set clear, achievable goals and work towards them.

Stay Committed: Some days will be harder than others. Remember why you started dancing and keep that passion alive.

attending workshops and camps

There's a whole world of dance out there beyond your regular classes. Have you ever thought about attending a dance workshop or camp? These extra-curricular dance activities are like hidden treasures waiting to be discovered. Let's explore why they are fantastic and how they can supercharge your dance journey!

1. New Styles, New Moves

. . .

First off, workshops and camps are amazing places to learn new dance styles. Maybe you've been doing ballet, but have you tried hip-hop? Or maybe jazz? Each style has its own flavor and steps, and learning them can be super exciting. It's like adding new dance languages to your vocabulary. Imagine being able to 'speak' ballet, tap, and hip-hop!

2. Learning from Different Instructors

Every teacher has a unique way of teaching and different experiences to share. When you attend workshops, you get the chance to learn from various instructors. This can be a game-changer! You might pick up a new way of doing a step or a cool routine that you've never thought of before.

3. Making New Friends Who Dance

Workshops and camps are social events too. You'll meet other kids who love dancing just as much as you do. These new friends can be from different places and backgrounds. Think about the fun dance moves you can learn from each other! Plus, making friends who share your passion is always cool.

4. Getting Inspired

At these events, you often get to see performances by experienced dancers and sometimes even professionals! Watching them can be super inspiring. It's like watching your favorite superheroes in action, but in dance! These experiences can fill you with new ideas and energy to bring back to your own dancing.

5. Building Confidence

Performing in front of new people or trying a dance style you're not used to can be scary at first. But guess what? It's also a great way to build your confidence. Each time you step out of your comfort zone, you become a braver, stronger dancer. And the cheers and claps at the end? Best feeling ever!

6. Learning to Adapt

Workshops and camps can be fast-paced with lots to learn in a short time. This teaches you to adapt quickly, a skill that's super important in dance (and in life, too!). You learn to catch on quickly, think on your feet, and go with the flow.

7. Focus on Dancing

Imagine a few days where your main job is just to dance. Sounds like a dream, right? At dance camps, you can immerse yourself completely in dance without the usual distractions. It's a time when you can focus on improving your skills, learning new things, and just enjoying dance to the fullest.

8. Health and Fitness

Dance is a great workout, and at these workshops and camps, you'll be moving a lot! This is great for your health and fitness. Think of it as exercise but with way more laughter, music, and fun.

9. Creating Memories

The experiences you have at these dance events create lasting memories. From that funny dance-off at the camp to the new pirouette trick you learned at a workshop, these memories become part of your dance story. And who knows? Someday, you might be telling these stories to other young dancers.

10. Fueling Your Passion

Sometimes, we all need a little extra spark to keep our passion for dance burning bright. Attending these extra activities can reignite your love for dance. It's like adding fuel to your dance fire, keeping you excited and motivated.

learning from others

Have you ever sat in front of a stage, mesmerized by the dancers, and thought, "Wow, I want to dance like them someday!"? Watching others dance, whether they're your peers, professionals, or even characters in a movie, isn't just fun—it's a super-important part of your dance journey. Let's dive into the magical world of learning from others!

1. Watching Performances: More Than Just Entertainment

When you watch a dance performance, it's like opening a book full of secrets. Each move, each expression tells a story, teaches a lesson. Have you seen the way a ballet dancer can tell a whole story just with their feet? Or how a hip-hop dancer can make it look like they're defying gravity? By watching these performances, you can pick up on these nuances. It's like learning a new language without even realizing it.

2. The Magic of Movement

Pay attention to how dancers move. Notice the little things: the way they point their toes, the fluidity of their arms, or the timing of their steps. These tiny details add up to make a dance spectacular. Try mimicking these movements. You might feel a bit silly at first, but that's how you learn!

3. Expression and Emotion

Dance isn't just about steps; it's about telling a story with your body. Watch how professional dancers express emotions. Are they happy, sad, excited, scared? See how their faces and bodies change with each emotion. This can inspire you to put more feeling into your own dancing.

4. Learning from Peers

Your friends and classmates in dance are also great teachers. Watch them when they dance. Everyone has something unique in their style. Maybe Anna has a way of spinning that keeps her from getting dizzy, or Jamal jumps in a way that makes him look like he's flying. You can learn so much just by observing your peers.

5. Constructive Feedback

When you watch others dance, you start to understand what looks good and what might need improvement. This can help you give and receive constructive feedback. It's not about saying, "That didn't look good." It's about saying, "That was cool, but maybe if you try this, it'll be even cooler!"

6. Inspiration and Creativity

Seeing different dancers and styles sparks creativity. You might see a move in a hip-hop routine that you want to try in jazz. Or you might get inspired to create your own dance. The possibilities are endless!

. . .

7. Understanding the Audience Perspective

Watching others helps you understand how an audience sees a dance. What catches your eye? What do you remember after the performance? This helps you think about how to make your own performances more engaging and memorable.

8. Professional Workshops and Masterclasses

If you get a chance, attend workshops or masterclasses by professional dancers. It's a great opportunity to see their techniques up close and even get some personalized tips. Plus, it's super exciting to meet dancers you look up to!

9. Dance as a Universal Language

Remember, dance is a universal language. Watching dancers from different cultures can teach you about the wide, wonderful world of dance. Each style from each country has its own story and history. It's like traveling the world without leaving your hometown.

10. Watching with a Critical Eye

As you watch more and grow in dance, you'll start to watch with a critical eye. This doesn't mean being judgmental. It means understanding what makes a dance effective, noticing the choreography, technique, and how dancers interact with the music and each other.

Beyond the Stage - Movies, TV, and Online Videos

You don't always have to go to a theater to watch great dancing. Dance movies, TV shows, and online videos are awesome resources. You can find tutorials, behind-the-scenes of professional rehearsals, and dance performances from all over the world. Watching these can be super fun and educational.

The Joy of Dance

Sarah Michaels

. . .

Remember, while it's great to learn and grow, the most important thing is to enjoy dance. Watching others should be fun and inspiring, not something that makes you stressed or worried about not being 'good enough'. Every dancer starts somewhere, and every dancer has something to learn, no matter how experienced they are.

9 /
the world of dance opportunities

competitions and performances

PICTURE THIS: the lights, the audience, the energy, and you, right in the middle of it all, ready to show what you've got. Sounds thrilling, doesn't it? Well, it absolutely is! But there's also a lot more to it. Let's explore together!

1. The Thrill of the Stage

When you step onto the stage for a competition or a recital, it feels like stepping into a new world. The spotlight, the music, and the audience's eyes all on you—it's a unique experience that you'll remember for a lifetime. It's normal to feel a bundle of nerves and excitement. That's part of the magic!

2. Preparing for the Big Day

Preparing for a performance or competition is

like preparing for an adventure. It involves lots of practice, but also planning your costume, understanding the stage layout, and knowing your routine inside out. It's not just about the steps; it's about being ready to adapt if something unexpected happens.

3. Teamwork in Group Performances

If you're performing in a group, you'll learn a lot about teamwork. Dancing with others requires synchrony, cooperation, and being aware of each other's movements. It's like being part of a dance family where everyone supports each other.

4. Solo Performances: A Personal Challenge

Performing solo? That's a different kind of challenge. It's just you and the music, expressing yourself through dance. It's a chance to show your personal style and tell your story. Remember, it's not just about impressing the audience; it's about expressing yourself.

5. The World of Dance Competitions

Dance competitions can range from local community events to big national contests. They're a place where dancers from different backgrounds come together. You'll see a variety of styles and meet dancers of all levels. It's a fantastic way to learn from others and get inspired.

6. Understanding Judging and Feedback

In competitions, judges provide feedback on your performance. This feedback is super valuable. It's not about winning or losing; it's about learning what you're doing well and what you can improve. Take this feedback as a guide to becoming a better dancer.

7. The Importance of Recitals

Recitals are a bit different from competitions. They're more about showcasing what you've learned, often in a less formal, more celebratory environment. It's a chance for your friends and family to see your progress and for you to enjoy the moment.

8. Handling Stage Fright

Feeling nervous? That's completely normal. Even professional dancers feel stage fright sometimes. The key is to channel that nervous energy into your performance. Deep breaths, positive thinking, and lots of practice can help keep those butterflies in check.

9. The Art of Makeup and Costumes

Costumes and makeup are a big part of performances and competitions. They help tell the story of your dance. Learning how to get your costume and makeup just right is another fun aspect of preparing for the stage.

10. Celebrating Your Achievements

After a performance or competition, take a moment to celebrate what you've achieved. Whether you win a trophy or not, you've accomplished something amazing. You've put in the work, faced your nerves, and performed in front of an audience. That's a big deal!

11. Learning and Growing

Every performance and competition is a learning experience. You'll find things you want to work on and things you're really proud of. That's the beauty of dance—it's a journey that's always evolving.

dance in education

From your school's auditorium to the halls of universities, there's a whole universe of dance waiting for you!

1. Dance Classes in School: More than Just Fun

Dance in school isn't just a break from math or science. It's a subject that helps you grow in so many ways. You learn about different cultures through their dances, work on your coordination, and even improve your teamwork skills. And yes, it's super fun, too!

2. School Performances and Events

Many schools have dance performances or

talent shows. Participating in these events is a fantastic way to showcase your skills. It's also a chance to work with teachers and classmates on something creative and exciting.

3. Dance as Physical Education

In some schools, dance is part of physical education. Here, you get to understand how your body moves, the importance of staying fit, and how dance can be a fun way to exercise. Who knew getting fit could be this enjoyable?

4. Cultural Celebrations and Dance

Schools often celebrate different cultures and festivals, and dance is a big part of these celebrations. This is your chance to explore dances from around the world, understand their history, and maybe even perform them!

5. After-School Dance Programs

Many schools offer after-school dance programs. These programs might cover different styles, from hip-hop to ballet. Joining these programs can help you find which style of dance sparks your interest the most.

6. Dance Competitions in School

Some schools participate in dance competitions. This can be an incredible experience. You'll learn about healthy competition, the joy of performing, and the thrill of working together towards a common goal.

7. The Role of Dance in Arts Education

Dance is a vital part of arts education. It helps you develop an appreciation for the arts and understand how dance can be a form of expression. Through dance, you get to tell stories without words, using your body as your paintbrush!

8. Dance in High School

High school can take your dance education to a new level. Here, you might have opportunities to join more advanced dance classes or be a part of larger, more elaborate productions. It's a great time to hone your skills and explore dance more seriously.

9. Scholarships for Young Dancers

If you're really passionate about dance, there are scholarships available to help young talents like you. These scholarships can support your training and even lead to opportunities in prestigious dance schools or programs.

10. Dance in Higher Education

For those dreaming big, dance in higher education, like colleges and universities, is an exciting path. Here, you can study dance in-depth, learn from experienced professionals, and even earn degrees in dance.

11. Career Paths in Dance

Studying dance can lead to various careers, not just as a dancer. You can become a choreographer, dance teacher, dance therapist, and more. The world of dance opens doors to so many possibilities.

career paths

The world of dance is not just about performing on stage; there are so many paths you can twirl, leap, and shuffle into. Let's explore the exciting career opportunities waiting for you in the fantastic world of dance!

1. Professional Performer

Becoming a professional dancer is a dream many of you might have. This means performing in ballets, contemporary dance companies, musical theater, TV shows, movies, or even as a backup dancer for music artists. It requires dedication, tons of practice, and a deep passion for dance.

2. Choreographer

If you love creating dance routines, think about becoming a choreographer. Choreographers design dance sequences for shows, movies, dance companies, and even individual performers. It's like being a painter, but instead of paint, you use movements to create beautiful pictures.

3. Dance Instructor

Teaching dance is another fabulous career. As a dance instructor, you could teach in schools, private dance studios, or even online! You get to share your love for dance with others and help them grow into amazing dancers.

4. Dance Therapist

Did you know that dance can be used for healing? Dance therapists use movement to help people emotionally and physically. They work in hospitals, schools, and various therapy centers. It's a career that combines dance with helping people - pretty cool, right?

5. Dance Company Director

A dance company director runs a dance group or company. This role involves a lot of planning, from choosing the dances and dancers to organizing performances. It's perfect for someone who loves to be in charge and has a vision for what they want in a performance.

6. Dance Critic or Journalist

For those who love writing and dance, becoming a dance critic or journalist could be your spotlight. You would write reviews of performances, interview dancers and choreographers, and report on the latest dance trends.

7. Dance Photographer or Videographer

If you have an eye for capturing moments, think about dance photography or videography. This career is all about taking stunning photos or videos of dancers and dance performances.

8. Costume Designer

Every dancer knows that costumes are a big part of a performance. As a costume designer, you get to create the outfits that help tell the story of the dance. It's a path that combines fashion and dance.

9. Dance Notator

Dance notators use a special form of writing to record dance movements. This way, dances can be preserved and taught to others exactly as they were intended. It's like being a historian for dance!

10. Stage Manager or Production Crew

Behind every great performance is an awesome stage crew. This includes stage managers, lighting and sound technicians, and set designers. They make sure everything runs smoothly during a performance.

11. Dance Fitness Instructor

Love dance and fitness? As a dance fitness instructor, you combine these passions. Teaching classes like Zumba or Barre, you help people stay fit while having a blast dancing.

12. Arts Administrator

Arts administrators make sure dance companies and arts organizations run effectively. They work on budgets, marketing, and organizing events. This job is perfect for someone who loves dance but also enjoys the business side of things.

10 / staying healthy and fit

nutrition for dancers

JUST LIKE A HIGH-PERFORMANCE car needs the right fuel to run at its best, your body needs the right food to help you dance your heart out!

Eating Like a Star: The Basics

You might think that dancers should eat very little to stay in shape, but that's a big myth. Dancers need energy, and energy comes from food. The trick is eating the right kinds of food in the right amounts.

Sarah Michaels

. . .

1. The Magic Trio: Carbs, Protein, and Fats

Carbs are Your Energy Fuel: Carbs are not your enemy! Whole grains, fruits, and vegetables are great sources of carbohydrates, which give you the energy to leap, twirl, and glide across the floor.

Proteins are Your Muscle Builders: After a long day of dancing, your muscles need to repair and grow. Lean meats, fish, beans, and nuts are great protein sources.

Fats Keep You Going: Healthy fats are essential, too. They help your body absorb vitamins and keep your energy levels steady. Avocados, olive oil, and nuts are excellent sources of healthy fats.

2. Don't Forget Your Vitamins and Minerals

Your body needs lots of different vitamins and minerals to stay healthy. Calcium and vitamin D are super important for strong bones – think dairy products, leafy greens, and fortified foods. Iron, which you can find in meats and leafy greens, keeps your blood healthy, and potassium, found in bananas and potatoes, helps prevent muscle cramps.

3. Hydration is Key

Water is your best friend. Dancing can be sweaty work, and it's super important to stay hydrated. Keep a water bottle with you and sip regularly, especially during practice.

Mealtime Tips for Dancers

Planning your meals and snacks can make a big difference in how you feel and dance.

Breakfast: Start your day with a good mix of carbs, protein, and a little fat. Think whole-grain toast with avocado and a side of scrambled eggs.

Lunch: Keep it balanced. A turkey sandwich on whole grain bread with a side salad is a great choice.

Dinner: After a day of dancing, your body needs to recover. Grilled chicken, steamed veggies, and brown rice can be a perfect meal to end your day.

Snacks: Choose snacks that give you energy without weighing you down. Yogurt, fruit, or a small handful of nuts are great choices.

Dance Competition and Performance Days

On big days like a competition or performance, eating right is super important.

Before the Performance: Eat a meal that's high in carbs and moderate in protein two to three hours before. You want energy, but you also don't want to feel heavy or full.

During the Event: Keep snacks like granola bars, fruit, or crackers handy for quick energy boosts.

After the Performance: Celebrate your hard work with a balanced meal. Your body will thank you for the nutrients to recover!

. . .

Listening to Your Body

Everybody is different, and it's important to listen to your own body. Some foods that work great for your friend might not feel good for you. It's okay to experiment and find out what food makes you feel the best.

fitness and cross-training

The more tools (or skills) you have, the better you can build (or dance)!

Why Is Fitness Important in Dance?

First things first, why should dancers even think about fitness outside of their regular dance classes? Well, think of your favorite dancer leaping across the stage. That strength and control don't just come from dance practice; they come from being fit and strong all around. Plus, being fit helps prevent injuries, and we all want to dance injury-free, right?

. . .

Cross-Training: What Is It?

Cross-training means doing different types of exercises that support and enhance your dancing. It's like adding extra flavors to your favorite dish to make it even more delicious!

1. Cardiovascular Exercises: Boost Your Stamina

What it is: Cardio exercises get your heart pumping and improve your endurance.

Why it's great for dancers: The more you work on your cardio, the longer you can dance without getting tired.

Fun cardio activities: Swimming, cycling, or even a game of tag with friends can be awesome cardio workouts.

2. Strength Training: Build Your Muscle Power

What it is: These exercises make your muscles stronger.

Why it's great for dancers: Strong muscles mean better lifts, jumps, and overall control in your movements.

Kid-friendly strength exercises: Push-ups, sit-ups, and squats can be done anywhere, anytime. No gym required!

3. Flexibility Training: Bend It Like a Pro

What it is: These exercises help you become more bendy and flexible.

Why it's great for dancers: Flexibility is key for those amazing kicks and splits.

Easy flexibility exercises: Yoga and simple stretching routines can work wonders for your flexibility.

4. Balance Training: Keep Steady On Your Feet

What it is: This training focuses on improving your balance.

Why it's great for dancers: Good balance is essential for pirouettes and maintaining poses.

Fun balance activities: Try standing on one foot or walking on a balance beam at the park.

Cross-Training Schedule for Young Dancers

Remember, balance is key. You shouldn't be doing cross-training exercises every day. Here's a simple plan:

Monday and Wednesday: Focus on strength training. This can be simple body-weight exercises.

Tuesday and Thursday: Work on your flexibility with some yoga or stretching routines.

Weekends: Have fun with some cardio activities. Maybe a bike ride or a swim?

Safety First!

It's super important to remember to do these exercises safely:

· · ·

Warm-Up: Always start with a warm-up to get your muscles ready.

Start Slow: Begin with easy exercises and gradually increase the difficulty.

Rest Days: Your body needs time to rest and recover. Make sure you take a break!

Listening to Your Body

Just like with dance, listen to your body when you do these exercises. If something hurts (in a bad way), stop and rest. It's all about keeping your body happy and healthy.

Cross-Training Fun With Friends

Doing these exercises with friends can make them even more fun. Why not invite a friend to bike with you or have a mini yoga session together?

Sarah Michaels

mental health

Just like a beautiful dance routine, taking care of your mind is an art, and it's crucial for every dancer!

Why Mental Health Matters in Dance

Dancing is not just about moving your feet and waving your arms. It's about expressing yourself, telling a story, and sharing emotions. That's why it's super important to take care of your mental health. When your mind is happy, your dance shines brighter!

Understanding Stress and Anxiety

Dancing can sometimes feel like riding a roller coaster, full of ups and downs. Before a performance or competition, you might feel butterflies in your stomach – that's normal! It's called performance anxiety, and guess what? Every dancer experiences it at some point.

. . .

Dealing With Performance Anxiety

Breathe Deep: When you feel nervous, take deep breaths. It helps calm your mind.

Positive Talk: Remind yourself of all the hard work you've put in. Tell yourself, "I can do this!"

Visualize Success: Close your eyes and imagine yourself nailing that routine. It's like a rehearsal in your mind.

Stay Prepared: Practicing your routine until you're confident can help reduce nerves.

The Pressure to Be Perfect

In dance, sometimes there's a lot of pressure to be perfect. But remember, nobody's perfect! Mistakes are how we learn and grow. Instead of getting down on yourself for a misstep, think of it as a step towards becoming even better.

Building a Positive Self-Image

How you see yourself in the mirror matters a lot. Always focus on the positives about yourself and your dancing. Celebrate your strengths and embrace your unique style!

Handling Criticism Constructively

Feedback is a big part of dance. Not all criticism is bad. Learn to take constructive criticism as a tool to improve. Remember, when someone offers advice, it's to help you grow, not to bring you down.

The Importance of Taking Breaks

. . .

Dance Your Dreams

Dancing non-stop without rest can be tough on your mind. It's important to take breaks. Do something fun outside of dance. Read a book, play a game, or just chill. Your brain will thank you for it!

Talk About Your Feelings

It's totally okay to talk about how you feel. Whether you're feeling super excited or a bit down, sharing your feelings with a friend, family member, or teacher can make a big difference. It's like opening a window in a stuffy room – it lets fresh air in.

Mindfulness and Meditation

Mindfulness and meditation are like secret superpowers for your brain. They help you stay calm, focused, and happy. Even just a few minutes a day can make a big difference. Try sitting quietly, focusing on your breath, and letting your thoughts float by like clouds.

. . .

Sarah Michaels

Fuel Your Body and Mind

Just like cars need the right fuel to run, your body and mind need healthy food to perform best. Eating a balanced diet keeps your energy levels up and your mind sharp.

Getting Enough Sleep

Never underestimate the power of a good night's sleep. Sleep helps your mind and body recover from a day full of dancing and learning. Aim for 8-10 hours of sleep – your body and mind will thank you in the morning!

Celebrating Your Progress

Remember to celebrate your achievements, no matter how small. Every step forward is a reason to be proud. Keep a diary or a journal of your dance journey. It's fun to look back and see how much you've achieved!

. . .

You Are Not Alone

If you're ever feeling too overwhelmed, remember, you are not alone. There's always someone ready to listen and help – a family member, a friend, a teacher, or even a professional counselor.

11 / your unique dance journey

THIS CHAPTER IS all about discovering and nurturing your unique dance style. Remember, every dancer has their own sparkle – it's time to find yours!

What is Your Dance Style?

Think of your dance style as your dance 'fingerprint'. It's special and unique to you! Whether it's the way you twirl, jump, or shake, your style is your own personal dance signature.

Discovering Your Style

Experiment with Different Styles: The world of dance is like a giant ice cream shop with endless flavors! Try hip-hop, ballet, tap, or jazz. Each one has its own rhythm and vibe.

Find Your Music Soul Mate: Dance and music are best friends. Explore different music genres.

You might find your body moves differently to hip-hop than it does to classical music.

Be Inspired, But Be You: It's great to have dance idols, but remember, you're not here to be a copycat. Pick up moves you love, then tweak them to make them your own.

Dance Freestyle: Just let the music take over and move however you feel. It's like doodling, but with your body!

Express Yourself

Your dance is a way to tell your story. Are you feeling super happy? Let your dance be light and bouncy. Feeling thoughtful? Maybe your movements become more slow and graceful.

Creativity in Choreography

Choreography is like painting, but instead of a brush, you use your body. Start with a simple step or move, then add your own twist. What if you do a spin before a jump? What if you reach higher, bend lower? Play around and see what happens.

Watch and Learn

Watch dancers perform – not just the famous ones, but anyone who catches your eye. Notice what you like about their style. Is it how they use their arms, or maybe their facial expressions? Gather ideas from everywhere.

Your Dance Diary

Keep a dance diary or sketchbook. Write down ideas for moves, draw stick figures, or jot down how different songs make you feel. It's your dance playground – have fun with it!

Costume and Appearance

Your outfit can be part of your style. Love bright colors? Wear them! Prefer cool and sleek? That's great too. Your costume can enhance your dance and help tell your story.

Confidence is Key

Sometimes the biggest challenge in creating your own style is feeling confident enough to show it off. Remember, every dancer has something special. Believe in your moves and others will too.

Ask for Feedback

Share your dance with friends, family, or your dance teacher. What do they think makes your dance unique? Sometimes others can see special things about our dance that we might not notice.

Perform Your Heart Out

When you get the chance to perform, give it your all. Your dance style isn't just about the moves; it's about how you perform them with emotion and energy.

Keep Growing and Evolving

Your style today might not be your style next year, and that's totally okay! As you grow, learn, and experience more, your dance style will change and evolve. That's the beauty of dance – it grows with you.

Embrace Mistakes

Mistakes are often where the best creativity comes from. Maybe you slip, but then find a cool new way to turn. Creativity often happens when things don't go as planned.

Stay True to Yourself

The most important part of your dance style is that it reflects YOU. Whether it's quirky, elegant, energetic, or chill, make sure it feels right. Your style should be a dance version of your personality.

By embracing your unique dance style, you're not just moving to music; you're telling the world who you are through your dance. There's no right or wrong in creative expression. Let your imagination lead your feet, and dance like nobody's watching. After all, the dance floor is your canvas – paint it with your moves, emotions, and style! Keep dancing, keep dreaming, and most importantly, keep being you!

Setting Long-Term Goals: How to envision and plan for your future in dance

12 / setting long-term goals - dream big and dance towards your future

HELLO, aspiring dancers! Today, let's dive into a really exciting topic - setting long-term goals for your dance journey. Just like a choreographer plans out a dance performance, planning your future in dance can be super fun and inspiring!

Dream Big, Start Small

Your dance dreams might be as high as the sky – and that's fantastic! Do you dream of being on a big stage? Teaching dance? Or mastering every dance style there is? Whatever it is, embrace it. But remember, every big dream starts with small steps.

Understanding Long-Term Goals

Long-term goals are like the top of a ladder. They're what you aim to reach after climbing all the smaller steps. These goals could be about where you want to be in dance in a year, five years, or even ten years!

Break It Down

Breaking down your big goals into smaller ones makes them less overwhelming. Think of it as learning a new dance routine. You don't try to learn the whole thing in one go, right? You learn it step by step.

Set S.M.A.R.T Goals

S.M.A.R.T stands for Specific, Measurable, Achievable, Relevant, and Time-bound. Let's break that down:

Specific: Be clear about what you want. Instead of saying, "I want to be a better dancer," say, "I want to master ballet turns."

Measurable: How will you know you've reached your goal? Maybe it's when you can do a perfect pirouette.

Achievable: Your goal should be challenging but possible. If you've just started dancing, setting a goal to be a professional dancer in a year might be a bit too ambitious.

Relevant: Your goals should matter to you and align with your overall dance dreams.

Time-bound: Set a deadline. Maybe you want to master those ballet turns in six months.

Write It Down

Writing down your goals makes them real. Create a 'Dance Dream Journal' and write them down. You can even draw or paste pictures to make it more fun.

Visualize Your Success

Imagine yourself achieving your goals. What does it feel like? What does it look like? Visualization is a powerful tool that can motivate and inspire you.

Action Plan

Now, for the exciting part - how will you achieve your goals? If your goal is to master a particular dance form, your action plan might include extra classes, practice at home, and watching tutorials.

Seek Guidance

Talk to your dance teacher, a mentor, or even a professional dancer about your goals. They can offer valuable advice and guidance.

Celebrate Small Wins

Every small step you achieve is a win. Celebrate it! Finished a tough dance class? Give yourself a high five! Mastered a new move? Do a little victory dance!

Stay Flexible

Sometimes, goals change, and that's okay. You might start learning one dance style and then fall in love with another. It's all part of your dance journey.

Balancing Dance and Life

Remember, while chasing your dance dreams is important, so is school, spending time with friends and family, and other hobbies. Find a balance that makes you happy.

Stay Positive and Patient

Achieving big goals takes time. There might be days when you feel stuck or like you're not improving. It's normal. Stay positive and patient. Progress in dance, just like in life, can take time.

Keep Learning and Growing

Dance is an ever-evolving art form. Keep learning new things, attending workshops, and watching performances. The more you learn, the more you grow.

The Power of Perseverance

There will be challenges, but remember, every great dancer faced challenges too. The key is to keep going, keep practicing, and never give up on your dreams.

Share Your Journey

Talk about your goals with friends who also love to dance. You can support and motivate each other. Plus, it's more fun to dream big together!

staying inspired

Just like a star that keeps shining in the night sky, your love for dance can keep glowing strong, no matter how many years pass.

The Journey Begins with Passion

Remember the first time you put on your dancing shoes? Or the first dance class you attended? There was a magical feeling, right? That's passion – the secret ingredient that makes dancing so special.

Change It Up

Doing the same dance moves and routines can sometimes feel a bit like having the same flavor of ice cream every single day. Exciting at first, but after a while, you might want something different. Try new dance styles, music, and routines to keep things fresh and exciting.

Set New Challenges

Just like in a video game where you reach new levels, set new challenges in your dance journey. This could be learning a difficult move, participating in a dance competition, or even choreographing your own dance.

Find Your Dance Heroes

Do you have a favorite dancer or choreographer? Watching professionals can be super inspiring! Their performances, stories, and achievements can motivate you to keep dancing and exploring.

Create a Dance Vision Board

Imagine a board filled with pictures of your dance dreams, goals, and inspirations. You can include photos of your favorite dancers, dance quotes, and even your own dance photos. It's a visual reminder of why you love dance.

Dance with Friends

Dancing alone is fun, but dancing with friends? That's a whole other level of awesome! Whether it's in class, at a workshop, or just in your living room, sharing your dance passion with friends can keep the excitement alive.

Share Your Love for Dance

Ever tried teaching a dance move to a friend or family member? Sharing your knowledge and passion for dance can reignite your own love for it. Plus, it's super fun to see others learn and enjoy dance because of you.

Take Breaks When Needed

Sometimes, taking a short break from dance can help rejuvenate your passion. Engage in other activities you love, and you might find yourself coming back to dance with even more excitement.

Write a Dance Diary

Have you thought about keeping a diary just for

your dance experiences? Write about your classes, what you learned, what you found challenging, and what you love about dance. Looking back on your progress and experiences can be really inspiring.

Attend Dance Shows and Movies

There's something magical about watching a live dance performance or a dance movie. It can give you new ideas and remind you why you love dance.

Remember the Fun

Dance is about expression, creativity, and most importantly, having fun! If you're ever feeling a little less passionate, remind yourself to find the fun in dance again.

Practice Gratitude

Take a moment sometimes to think about how wonderful it is to be able to dance. Being grateful for your ability to dance, your teachers, and your dance friends can help you appreciate and love dance even more.

Explore the History of Dance

Learning about the history of dance and how it has evolved can be fascinating. Understanding the stories behind different dance styles can deepen your appreciation and passion for dance.

Join Online Dance Communities

There are so many dancers around the world sharing their love for dance online. Joining these communities can be a great way to stay inspired and connected.

Set Personal Performance Goals

Maybe you want to perform in front of your family, at a school event, or even on a bigger stage. Setting such goals can keep you motivated and excited about dancing.

Reflect on Your Dance Journey

Take some time to think about how far you've come in your dance journey. Remembering your achievements and growth can be a huge inspiration booster.

Help Others Discover Dance

Inspiring others to start dancing can reignite your own passion. Seeing someone else fall in love with dance because of you is an amazing feeling.

conclusion: the dance continues

reflecting on the journey

Let's take a moment to do something really important – let's turn around and look back at the journey we've been on. It's like climbing a mountain and pausing to see how far up you've come. It's not just about reaching the top; it's about remembering and cherishing every step you took to get there.

The First Steps

Remember the first time you stepped into a dance class? You might have been a bundle of nerves, excitement, or maybe a bit of both. Think about that younger you, taking those brave first steps. How did it feel? Scary? Fun? All of these memories are precious gems in your dance journey.

Conclusion: The Dance Continues

Overcoming Challenges

There have been times when learning a new dance move felt like trying to solve a super hard puzzle, right? Maybe there were days when you thought, "I just can't get this right!" But guess what? You didn't give up! You practiced, you persevered, and you overcame those challenges. That's something to be really proud of.

The Joy of Learning

Dance is like a language without words. Think about all the cool moves and styles you've learned. Each one tells a story, expresses an emotion, and adds more words to your dance vocabulary. What has been your favorite dance style or move so far?

The Power of Performance

Performing in front of others, whether it's in a recital, a competition, or just for family, is a big part of your journey. Do you remember your first performance? How did you feel? Nervous? Excited? Each performance is a milestone in your journey, marking your growth as a dancer and as a person.

Friendships Made Along the Way

In your dance journey, you've probably met many other dancers. Some may have become close friends. These friendships are special because they're built on shared experiences, mutual encouragement, and a common love for dance.

Learning from Mistakes

Mistakes are like the secret sauce to getting better at anything, including dance. Think about a time when something didn't go as planned in your dancing. What did you learn from that experience? How did it help you grow?

The Support Team

Your journey hasn't been a solo one. There are teachers, family, and friends who have supported you all along. Reflect on how they've helped you. Maybe it's a teacher who gave you extra help, or a family member who always cheered the loudest for you.

Exploring Creativity

Dance is a wonderful way to express yourself creatively. Have you ever made up your own dance routine or experimented with creating unique moves? These moments of creativity are an exciting part of your journey.

Discovering Yourself

Dancing isn't just about moving to music; it's also a journey of self-discovery. Through dance, you learn about your strengths, your passions, and even your limits. What are some things you've discovered about yourself through dance?

Conclusion: The Dance Continues

Celebrating the Achievements

Let's not forget to celebrate your achievements, big and small! Every step forward is worth celebrating. Whether it's nailing a difficult move, improving your flexibility, or just gaining more confidence, these achievements are markers of your progress.

The Transformative Power of Dance

Dance can transform us in so many ways. It makes us stronger, more disciplined, and more confident. How do you feel dance has transformed you? Maybe you're more outgoing now, or you've found a new way to express your emotions.

The Never-Ending Journey

The beautiful thing about dance is that there's always more to learn, more to explore. Your journey doesn't really have an end; it evolves with you. You grow, your dance grows, and the journey continues.

Looking Ahead

While it's great to look back and reflect, it's also exciting to look ahead. What are your dreams and goals for the future in dance? Maybe you want to learn a new style, perform on a bigger stage, or even teach others one day.

The Legacy You're Creating

Every dancer creates their own legacy, their

own story. Think about what you want your dance story to say. What do you want to be remembered for in your dance journey? This is the legacy you're building with every step, spin, and leap.

Gratitude for the Journey

Take a moment to feel grateful for your dance journey. It's a unique path that has shaped you in so many wonderful ways. Be thankful for the experiences, the lessons, and the joy it's brought into your life.

future aspirations

Let's talk about how you can dream big and turn those dreams into a reality. The world of dance is vast and bright, and it's waiting for you to make your mark!

The Power of Big Dreams

What does it mean to dream big? It means imagining your future in the most amazing way possible. It's like when you close your eyes and picture yourself dancing on the biggest stages, creating awe-inspiring routines, or even teaching others to dance. Big dreams are the seeds from which great achievements grow.

Believe in Yourself

The first step in making your dreams come true

Conclusion: The Dance Continues

is believing in yourself. Believe that you can achieve great things in dance. Remember, every famous dancer once started as a beginner, just like you. They reached their dreams because they believed they could, and you can too!

Set Your Sights High

What are your biggest dreams when it comes to dance? Do you want to become a professional ballet dancer, a hip-hop choreographer, or maybe even start your own dance school? Write down your dreams. Seeing them on paper makes them more real and achievable.

Learn, Learn, and Learn Some More

The path to your dreams is paved with learning and practice. Keep learning new dance styles, techniques, and methods. The more you learn, the better equipped you'll be to achieve your big dreams. Remember, knowledge in dance is like a treasure chest that keeps on giving.

Seek Inspiration

Look for inspiration everywhere. Watch performances by dance legends, read stories about successful dancers, and listen to music that moves your soul. Inspiration is like fuel for your dreams. It lights up your imagination and keeps your passion burning.

Setting Goals

Conclusion: The Dance Continues

Dreams become achievable when you break them down into goals. Set small goals that lead to your big dream. Maybe your first goal is to master a particularly tricky dance move or perform a solo at your next recital. Each goal you achieve brings you closer to your dream.

Hard Work and Dedication

Achieving big dreams in dance requires hard work and dedication. There will be days when you feel tired or discouraged, but remember your dream and why you started dancing. Let your love for dance be the strength that keeps you going.

Overcoming Obstacles

The journey to your dreams might not always be smooth. You'll face challenges and obstacles along the way. But guess what? Overcoming these challenges will make you stronger and more determined. Every obstacle you overcome is a victory on the path to your dream.

Staying Healthy and Fit

To keep dancing towards your dreams, it's important to stay healthy and fit. A balanced diet, regular exercise, and adequate rest are crucial. Take care of your body, as it's your most important tool in achieving your dance dreams.

Finding Support

Share your dreams with family, friends, and

teachers. Their support, advice, and encouragement can be incredibly valuable. Sometimes, just talking about your dreams can make them feel more achievable.

The Journey is Part of the Dream

Remember, the journey towards your dream is just as important as the dream itself. Cherish every practice, every performance, and every learning opportunity. These experiences are the building blocks of your future in dance.

Visualize Your Success

Visualize yourself achieving your dreams. Picture yourself performing on stage, winning a competition, or teaching a class. Visualization is a powerful tool that can help turn your dreams into reality.

Embrace Opportunities

Be on the lookout for opportunities that can lead you to your dreams. This might be attending a dance workshop, auditioning for a role, or participating in a competition. Opportunities are doors that lead to new paths on your dream journey.

The Importance of Balance

While chasing your dreams, don't forget to enjoy other aspects of life too. Spend time with friends, enjoy your hobbies, and have fun. Balance is key to a happy and fulfilling journey in dance.

Conclusion: The Dance Continues

Creating Your Own Path

Your dance journey is unique, and your path to your dreams may be different from others. Don't be afraid to create your own path, to try new things, and to follow your heart.

Never Give Up

No matter what, never give up on your dreams. With passion, hard work, and determination, you can achieve anything you set your mind to. Believe in the magic of your dreams – they are the stars guiding you in the dance of life.

The Dance of Dreams

Your journey in dance is like a beautiful, endless dance – full of twists, turns, leaps, and bounds. With each step you take, you're moving closer to your dreams. Keep dancing with all your heart, and one day, you'll look back and realize you're living the dream you once only imagined.

Dream big, dance passionately, and let your heart lead the way. Your future in dance is a canvas waiting for your unique colors. Paint it with your dreams, your passion, and your dedication. The stage is yours, the music is playing – now go out there and show the world the magic you can create with your dance!

Conclusion: The Dance Continues

final words of wisdom

Dancing is not just about the steps or the music; it's about expressing yourself. Let your heart lead the way. Whether you're on stage or in the studio, dance like nobody's watching. Let your emotions flow through your movements and create something beautiful that is uniquely yours.

The Importance of Practice

Never underestimate the power of practice. Even when it seems hard, and you feel like you're not making progress, trust in the process. Every practice session is like a puzzle piece, helping to complete the beautiful picture of your dance journey. Remember, the most accomplished dancers are those who dedicate time to perfect their craft.

Embrace Every Opportunity

Life will offer you many opportunities to dance, learn, and grow. Embrace them with open arms. Whether it's a new style of dance, a chance to perform, or even a workshop, each experience adds to your skill, confidence, and love for dance.

Dealing with Challenges

Challenges are part of every dancer's journey. There will be tough days, but they are there to teach you and make you stronger. Approach each challenge with courage and determination. Every

Conclusion: The Dance Continues

challenge you overcome is a triumph, a reason to be proud.

Find Your Support Circle

Remember, you're not alone on this dance journey. Surround yourself with people who support and believe in you – family, friends, teachers, and fellow dancers. They are your cheerleaders, your advisers, and sometimes, your shoulder to lean on.

Stay Curious and Keep Learning

Dance is a world of endless learning. Stay curious and hungry for knowledge. Learn from your teachers, your peers, and even from dancers you admire from afar. Each piece of knowledge is a tool that helps you become a better dancer.

Take Care of Yourself

Your body and mind are the most important instruments you have in dance. Take good care of them. Eat healthily, get enough sleep, and find time to relax. Remember, a happy, healthy dancer is a successful dancer.

Celebrate Every Achievement

Celebrate your achievements, no matter how small they seem. Mastered a new move? Celebrate! Completed a tough routine? Celebrate! Every achievement is a step forward in your dance journey, and every step deserves recognition.

The Beauty of Teamwork

Conclusion: The Dance Continues

Dancing can be both a solo and a team effort. Learn to work well with others. Be kind, respectful, and supportive. The friendships and connections you make through dance are just as precious as the skills you learn.

Handling Criticism Gracefully

Feedback and criticism can help you grow, even if it sometimes feels tough. Listen, learn, and use it to improve. Remember, constructive criticism is not a sign of failure; it's a stepping stone to success.

Stay True to Yourself

In a world full of different dance styles and influences, it's important to stay true to yourself. Embrace your unique style and personality. Your individuality is what makes you a special dancer.

Never Stop Dreaming

Keep dreaming big. Your dreams are the stars guiding your journey in dance. They give you direction and purpose. Hold onto them tightly, and believe that you have the power to make them come true.

Enjoy the Journey

Dancing is a journey, not just a destination. Enjoy every moment of it – the highs, the lows, the learning, and the growing. The joy you find in dance is something that will stay with you for a lifetime.

Conclusion: The Dance Continues

The Power of Resilience

Learn to bounce back from setbacks. Resilience is a powerful trait in a dancer. It's not about never falling; it's about getting back up every time you do. Each time you pick yourself up, you become stronger and more determined.

Keep the Passion Alive

Never lose that spark, that passion for dance. It's the fire that drives you, that keeps you moving forward. Let that passion shine in every step, every leap, and every spin.

And Finally, Dance for Joy

At the end of the day, dance because it brings you joy. Let it be your celebration of life, your expression of happiness. When you dance for joy, you light up the world around you.

appendices

glossary of dance terms

1. Arabesque: This is a pose where a dancer stands on one leg while the other leg is extended straight behind. It's like you're a majestic bird with one wing stretching out behind you.

2. Balancé: It's a rocking step that's really fun! The dancer shifts their weight from one foot to the other, and it kind of feels like swaying to a sweet melody.

3. Chaîné Turns: These are super quick and exciting turns. Imagine spinning around rapidly, one turn after another, like you're a merry-go-round!

4. Demi-plié: This means a small or half bending

Appendices

of the knees. Think of it as a gentle dip, like you're preparing to jump high or land softly.

5. Elevé: It's a rise up onto the balls of the feet from flat feet. Imagine you're trying to reach for a star, standing tall on your tiptoes.

6. Fondu: It's a smooth bending of your standing leg, kind of like you're melting into a chocolate fondue!

7. Glissade: This term means to glide. It's a smooth step from one foot to the other, like you're floating across the floor.

8. Jeté: A leap from one foot to the other. Think of it like you're a playful dolphin leaping out of the water.

9. Pas de bourrée: A quick, behind-side-front three-step movement. It's a little like you're tiptoeing sneakily but gracefully.

10. Pirouette: It's a turn on one leg with the other leg in passé (knee bent so your foot is near the standing leg's knee). Imagine you're a spinning top, whirling around elegantly.

11. Relevé: A rise onto the toes. Think of a majestic mountain peak; that's how high and strong you stand.

12. Sauté: This means jump in French. It's like you're a kangaroo hopping energetically.

13. Tendu: Stretching the leg and foot out from

the body and then sliding it back. Picture drawing a straight line on the floor with your toe.

14. Attitude: A pose with one leg lifted and bent at a 90-degree angle, either in front or behind. You're like a thoughtful sculpture, striking a pose.

15. Cambré: It's a bend of the body to the side or back. Think of a beautiful willow tree, bending gracefully in the breeze.

16. Pas de chat: Meaning 'step of the cat,' it's a jump where you bend both knees and lift them up, like a cat leaping softly.

17. Rond de jambe: It means 'circle of the leg.' Picture drawing circles on the floor or in the air with your toe, like a fancy painter.

18. Grand battement: A big kick or beat, where you lift the leg high up and then bring it back down. It's like you're a drum major, leading a parade with high kicks.

19. Piqué: It means to prick and is often used for a turn where you step directly onto the pointe or demi-pointe. Imagine you're stepping over puddles, quickly and lightly.

20. En croix: This term means 'in the shape of a cross.' It refers to doing a dance step to the front, side, and back in a cross pattern.

Appendices

directory of dance resources

1. Dance Schools and Studios:

The Juilliard School (New York City, USA): A world-renowned school offering top-notch dance programs. Imagine learning ballet, modern, and contemporary dance in the heart of New York City!

Paris Opera Ballet School (Paris, France): A dream place for ballet lovers! It's one of the oldest and most prestigious ballet schools globally.

Pineapple Dance Studios (London, UK): Famous for its diverse dance classes, from street dance to jazz, it's a hub for those looking to try different styles.

Local Dance Studios: Don't forget to check out local studios in your area. They might offer great classes in everything from hip-hop to tap dance.

2. Online Dance Platforms:

Stepping with YouTube: There are channels like Just Dance or 1MILLION Dance Studio, where you can learn cool routines right from your home.

Virtual Dance Classes: Websites like DancePlug or CLI Studios offer virtual classes with famous instructors. Perfect for dancing in your living room!

Dance Apps: Apps like STEEZY or Dance Reality can guide you with step-by-step instructions and augmented reality experiences.

Appendices

3. Dance Books for Inspiration and Learning:

"A Child's Introduction to Ballet" by Laura Lee: This book comes with stories, music, and illustrations – perfect for beginning dancers.

"The Young Dancer" by Darcey Bussell: Written by a former principal dancer of The Royal Ballet, this book offers great insights into ballet technique and history.

"Dance Anatomy" by Jacqui Greene Haas: If you're curious about how your body moves in dance, this book is fantastic, filled with illustrations and explanations.

4. Captivating Dance Documentaries:

"First Position": Follow young ballet dancers as they prepare for the Youth America Grand Prix, one of the world's most prestigious ballet competitions.

"Pina": A tribute to the late choreographer Pina Bausch, this film uses beautiful imagery to showcase modern dance.

"Step Up Revolution: Dance Workout": A fun way to learn dance and stay fit, inspired by the famous "Step Up" movie series.

5. Online Dance Communities:

Dance Forums and Blogs: Websites like Dance.net or Dance Spirit magazine's site offer a

Appendices

platform where you can discuss dance, get advice, and read about dance experiences.

Social Media Groups: Platforms like Facebook have numerous dance groups where you can connect with other dancers, share videos, and get feedback.

6. Dancewear and Equipment:

Local Dancewear Stores: Check out your local dancewear shop for things like leotards, tights, and shoes.

Online Retailers: Websites like Discount Dance Supply or Capezio offer a wide range of dance gear that you can order from home.

7. Dance Festivals and Workshops:

Summer Intensives: Many professional companies and schools offer summer programs, like the American Ballet Theatre's Summer Intensive.

Local Workshops: Keep an eye out for workshops in your community. They are a great way to learn from different instructors and styles.

8. Dance Competitions and Performance Opportunities:

Youth America Grand Prix: A fantastic ballet competition for young dancers.

Local Theater Productions: Joining local theater or community dance productions can be a great way to gain performance experience.

Milton Keynes UK
Ingram Content Group UK Ltd.
UKHW021647201124
451457UK00008B/170